ISBN : 9798388053206
First edition, 2023

The Importance of Inspirational Leadership in Fostering Growth and Success

Through 10 years of experience and research, it has become clear to me that inspirational leadership is the cornerstone of effective and sustainable leadership. At its core, inspirational leadership is about motivating and empowering others to achieve their full potential. It's about leading by example, setting a clear vision and direction, and fostering a culture of growth and learning.

Inspirational leaders understand the power of positive energy, and they work tirelessly to cultivate a sense of purpose and passion among their team members. They recognize that every individual has unique strengths and talents, and they strive to create an environment where everyone can thrive. Inspirational leaders lead from the heart, and they're not afraid to show vulnerability or express empathy for their team members.

One of the most important traits of an inspirational leader is the ability to communicate effectively. They know how to tell stories, articulate their vision, and inspire others with their words. They're also excellent listeners, and they seek out feedback and ideas from their team members. Inspirational leaders know that effective communication is a two-way street, and they're always looking for ways to improve their own communication skills.

Inspirational leadership is about creating a culture of excellence, where every individual feels valued, empowered, and inspired to achieve their full potential. It's about leading with authenticity, empathy, and a sense of purpose, and cultivating a shared vision that inspires others to take action. As a leader, your ultimate goal should be to inspire others to greatness, and to create a legacy of leadership that will endure for years to come.

#1 « From the very first, it has been the educated and intelligent of the Negro people that have led and elevated the mass, and the sole obstacles that nullified and retarded their efforts were slavery and race prejudice; for what is slavery but the legalized survival of the unfit and the nullification of the work of natural internal leadership?» - W. E. B. Du Bois

#2 « Today a reader, tomorrow a leader.» - Margaret Fuller

#3 « If I come in, and you're an employer, and I say, 'Well, I was a sniper in the Marine Corps. Do you have any sniper positions open?' 'No.' But if I told you that I was good at communication, good at leadership under stressful environments, team management, personnel management, leadership, being prompt, are stuff that I can bring to the table.» - Dakota Meyer

#4 « In this age, I don't care how tactically or operationally brilliant you are: if you cannot create harmony - even vicious harmony - on the battlefield based on trust across service lines, across coalition and national lines, and across civilian/military lines, you need to go home, because your leadership is obsolete.» - Jim Mattis

#5 « Such manifestations I account as representing the creative leadership of the new forces of thought and appreciation which attend changes in technological pattern and therefore of the pattern of human relationships in society.» - John Grierson

#6 « Make the right decision even when no one is watching, especially when no one is watching, and you will always turn out okay.» - Kim Kaupe

#7 « No matter how good you think you are as a leader, my goodness, the people around you will have all kinds of ideas for how you can get better. So for me, the most fundamental thing about leadership is to have the humility to continue to get feedback and to try to get better - because your job is to try to help everybody else get better.» - Jim Yong Kim

#8 « The highest calling of leadership is to challenge the status quo and unlock the potential of others. We need a leader who will lead the resurgence of this great nation and unlock its potential once again.» - Carly Fiorina

#9 « I am endlessly fascinated that playing football is considered a training ground for leadership, but raising children isn't. Hey, it made me a better leader: you have to take a lot of people's needs into account; you have to look down the road. Trying to negotiate getting a couple of kids to watch the same TV show requires serious diplomacy.» - Dee Dee Myers

#10 « True leadership isn't about having an idea. It's about having an idea and recruiting other people to execute on this vision.» - Leila Janah

#11 « There are good leaders who actively guide and bad leaders who actively misguide. Hence, leadership is about persuasion, presentation and people skills.» - Shiv Khera

#12 « I think the U.S. should assert its leadership in a more effective way.» - Sebastian Pinera

#13 « Leadership can not be measured in a poll or even in the result of an election. It can only be truly seen with the benefit of time. From the perspective of 20 years, not 20 days.» - Marco Rubio

#14 « Do not follow where the path may lead. Go instead where there is no path and leave a trail.» - Harold McAlindon

#15 « I can't change the direction of the wind, but I can adjust my sails to always reach my destination.» - Jimmy Dean

#16 « An old African leader says about leadership, he says that leadership should never be shared; it should always remain in the hands of the dispossessed people. We will lead the revolution.» - H. Rap Brown

#17 « You have to enable and empower people to make decisions independent of you. As I've learned, each person on a team is an extension of your leadership; if they feel empowered by you they will magnify your power to lead.» - Tom Ridge

#18 « Clearly you need a new team to go out to bat on your behalf; to fight for your rights and to report back to you personally and to the leadership of the IFP.» - Mangosuthu Buthelezi

#19 « In Britain, you do your job. When you do an American TV show, there is a sense of being one with the crew, and there is a leadership element, which was a learning curve for me because it is very different culturally. In Britain, you just do it, leave and say, 'Thanks.' » - Theo James

#20 « Yes, America must do the right thing, but to provide moral leadership, America must do it in the right way, too.» - David Cameron

#21 « It's not a matter of if economies around the world becoming low-carbon, but when and how: through struggle and strife or through advancement and progressive leadership. Larry Elliot described it today as the 'Green New Deal.' It's a leadership we in Britain can provide, and from which our economy can benefit.» - Lucy Powell

#22 « Al Qaeda is not the organization now that it was before. It is under stress organizationally. Its leadership spends more time trying to figure out how to keep from getting caught than they do trying to launch operations.» - Cofer Black

#23 « Lack of direction, not lack of time, is the problem. We all have twenty» - four hour days. - Zig Ziglar

#24 « The conductor is the artistic leader and sometimes cultural arbiter of his or her community. It is their leadership that is looked to and should anything go wrong, they are the persons taking most of the heat.» - Leonard Slatkin

#25 « The function of leadership is to produce more leaders, not more followers.» - Ralph Nader

#26 « There are three essentials to leadership: humility, clarity and courage.» - Fuchan Yuan

#27 « The Congress leadership always denied responsibilities to me both within the government and within the party organisation... They would always tell me my image as a Hindu leader was a constraint on my capacity as a political leader.» - Satpal Maharaj

#28 « A quiet conscience makes one strong!» - Anne Frank

#29 « The President's speech suggested to me that were we to follow his leadership, we will be in Iraq not for months, but for years. I also hope I am wrong on this.» - Daniel Inouye

#30 « When it comes to serious cuts to major programs like Medicaid, the American people are not calling for leadership but magic. They want cuts with no pain.» - Juan Williams

#31 « I am not saying that during the Second World War Germany did not, under the leadership of the National Socialist government, commit crimes.» - Ernst Zundel

#32 « Women in leadership cannot cry without raising a storm of commentary.» - Madeleine M. Kunin

#33 « President Reagan was a leader at a time when the American people most needed leadership. He outlined a vision that captured the imagination of the free world, a vision that toppled the Communist empire and freed countless millions.» - Dennis Hastert

#34 « Libertarians believe that any government interference is bad. Anyone with a brain knows that climate change needs governmental leadership, and they can smell this is bad news for their philosophy. Their ideology is so strongly held that, remarkably, it's overcoming the facts.» - Jeremy Grantham

#35 « A genuine leader is not a searcher for consensus but a moulder of consensus.» - Martin Luther King, Jr.

#36 « To succeed, one must be creative and persistent.» - John H. Johnson

#37 « You can't lead anyone else further than you have gone yourself.» - Gene Mauch

#38 « Whatever you are, be a good one.» - Abraham Lincoln

#39 « Management is nothing more than motivating other people.» - Lee Iacocca

#40 « We have to forget the past. History is something that even today we are paying the consequences, and the future is integration. We all as a people, as citizens, as the leadership of both countries should be looking in that direction.» - Atifete Jahjaga

#41 « We have two ears and one mouth so that we can listen twice as much as we speak.» - Epictetus

#42 « Remember that not getting what you want is sometimes a wonderful stroke of luck.» - Dalai Lama

#43 « Under Todd Haimes' leadership, Roundabout created a black-box theater whose sole mission was to house premieres by writers who are just starting out and have zero name recognition.» - Stephen Karam

#44 « A man who wants to lead the orchestra must turn his back on the crowd.» - Max Lucado

#45 « From a parent's right to know what their children are doing, to protecting citizens across the country from the growing threat of gang violence, the House Democrat leadership is simply out to lunch.» - Virginia Foxx

#46 « Leadership is the key to 99 per cent of all successful efforts.» - Erskine Bowles

#47 « I think what actually works best is local-level individual targeting of key leadership nodes.» - John Abizaid

#48 « I think national issues play into gubernatorial races less than, obviously, in Senate and Congressional races. Much less. They tend to be more decided by personality, leadership qualities and by state or local issues. They still have some effect, no question about it, but not as much as Senate and Congressional races.» - Ed Rendell

#49 « Digitas is a company that's very rapidly changing - the digital world changes every day. It's important we hire people who are curious about what's going on and who are willing to learn and want to learn. I look for core leadership traits.» - Laura Lang

#50 « I think President Obama could have handled politics and policies differently. But he has been decisive, strong, and consistent - important qualities in a president. Mitt Romney is indeed an Etch A Sketch, the antithesis of leadership.» - Eliot Spitzer

#51 « President Bush offers the American people an optimistic vision and a clear choice in November. The President has provided steady leadership in remarkably changing times. He knows exactly where he wants to lead this country, and he has complete confidence in the American people.» - Henry Bonilla

#52 « How we think shows through in how we act. Attitudes are mirrors of the mind. They reflect thinking.» - David Joseph Schwartz

#53 « Effective leadership is not about making speeches or being liked; leadership is defined by results not attributes.» - Peter Drucker

#54 « Those who let things happen usually lose to those who make things happen.» - Dave Weinbaum

#55 « It can be read in an afternoon, but you'll be re» - reading it for the rest of your life. - Eric S. Yuan

#56 « As the leadership team, we're taking bold and decisive action to evolve our organization and culture. This includes difficult steps, but they are necessary to position Microsoft for future growth and industry leadership.» - Amy Hood

#57 « I am the wealthiest man, not just in Europe, but in the whole world. I collect emotions. I am wealthy in that the people of Russia have twice entrusted me with the leadership of a great nation such as Russia - I believe that is my greatest wealth.» - Vladimir Putin

#58 « America is a great power possessed of tremendous military might and a wide-ranging economy, but all this is built on an unstable foundation which can be targeted, with special attention to its obvious weak spots. If America is hit in one hundredth of these weak spots, God willing, it will stumble, wither away and relinquish world leadership.» - Osama bin Laden

#59 « People who are truly strong lift others up. People who are truly powerful bring others together.» - Michelle Obama

#60 « In the military, I learned that 'leadership' means raising your hand and volunteering for the tough, important assignments.» - Tulsi Gabbard

#61 « Where there is an absence of international political leadership, civil society should step in to fill the gap, providing the energy and vision needed to move the world in a new and better direction.» - Daisaku Ikeda

#62 « We are what we pretend to be, so we must be careful about what we pretend to be.» - Kurt Vonnegut

#63 « Fortune always favors the brave, and never helps a man who does not help himself.» - P. T. Barnum

#64 « A significant number of pages and sentences that the administration wants to keep in a classified status have already been released publicly, some of it by public statements of the leadership of the CIA and the FBI.» - Bob Graham

#65 « But among you it will be different. Whoever wants to be a leader among you must be your servant.» - Matthew 20:26

#66 « We need fresh, new leadership with bold ideas and a new approach to get more people back to work with quality jobs and restored dignity in the lives of our Utahns.» - Scott Howell

#67 « High expectations are the key to everything.» - Sam Walton

#68 « If one has no compass, when one doesn't know where one stands and where one wants to go, one can deduce that one has no leadership or interest in shaping events.» - Helmut Kohl

#69 « The biggest difference is in the leadership. It was better for us. We had more coaches and mentors to help us. A lot of the younger players today suffer from a lack of direction.» - Isaiah Thomas

#70 « Self» - awareness and self

#71 « Good management is the art of making problems so interesting and their solutions so constructive that everyone wants to get to work and deal with them.» - Paul Hawken

#72 « Year after year, President Bush has broken his campaign promises on college aid. And year after year, the Republican leadership in Congress has let him do it.» - Sherrod Brown

#73 « Clearly no one knows what leadership has gone undiscovered in women of all races, and in black and other minority men.» - Gloria Steinem

#74 « In order to cultivate a set of leaders with legitimacy in the eyes of the citizenry, it is necessary that the path to leadership be visibly open to talented and qualified individuals of every race and ethnicity.» - Sandra Day O'Connor

#75 « Aim for the moon. If you miss, you may hit a star.» - W. Clement Stone

#76 « One of the tests of leadership is the ability to recognize a problem before it becomes an emergency.» - Arnold Glasow

#77 « In the midst of conflict, I was pushed to step forward. There were groups who wanted to change our leadership immediately. Some tried to force me to take over, but I rejected them.» - Suharto

#78 « There are many things that matter much more than an editor's gender in shaping the direction of the leadership.» - Nancy Gibbs

#79 « I talked about the need for American leadership, I talked about the importance of the United States to a more peaceful world, a world that has been quite turbulent in recent years, and needs a strong American anchor.» - Condoleezza Rice

#80 « So he shepherded them according to the integrity of his heart, And guided them with his skillful hands.» - Psalms 78:72

#81 « The growth and development of people is the highest calling of leadership.» - Harvey Firestone

#82 « In our family business, the Edelman children must earn their way - there were and will be no promises without performance and leadership. That may lead to some skinned knees, but it is certainly the best way to learn life lessons.» - Richard Edelman

#83 « We have treated our most serious adversaries, such as Iran and North Korea, in the most juvenile manner - by giving them the silent treatment. In so doing, we have weakened, not strengthened, our bargaining position and our leadership.» - Theodore C. Sorensen

#84 « 'Persistence prevails when all else fails.'» - Unknown

#85 « Rightwing organizations like Turning Point USA or Leadership Institute spend considerable amounts of money and time to train students with conservative values how to 'fight back.'« - Anthea Butler

#86 « One measure of leadership is the calibre of people who choose to follow you.» - Dennis A. Peer

#87 « But the person who scored well on an SAT will not necessarily be the best doctor or the best lawyer or the best businessman. These tests do not measure character, leadership, creativity, perseverance.» - William Julius Wilson

#88 « It's an American worker's right to unionize for sure, but that being said, don't expect me not to point out when or if union leadership takes advantage of union members.» - Joe Wurzelbacher

#89 « Leadership and punching above your weight doesn't necessarily always have to mean gunboat diplomacy and bombing other countries into the stone age. It can actually mean leading by example, and helping other countries.» - Clive Lewis

#90 « I think one of the keys to leadership is recognizing that everybody has gifts and talents. A good leader will learn how to harness those gifts toward the same goal.» - Ben Carson

#91 « Jamal Crawford reminds me the most of myself, the way he goes to the basket. But they need leadership.» - Earl Monroe

#92 « It is better to lead from behind and to put others in front, especially when you celebrate victory when nice things occur. You take the front line when there is danger. Then people will appreciate your leadership.» - Nelson Mandela

#93 « So, President Obama wants to change America. I understand that. We don't need to change America. We need to change the White House. We need to change the leadership in the White House.» - Mario Diaz-Balart

#94 « I want to deploy the leadership to meet the challenges that face us and to restore America's greatness.» - Paul Tsongas

#95 « I am not afraid of an army of lions led by a sheep; I am afraid of an army of sheep led by a lion.» - Alexander The Great

#96 « A good leader takes a little more than his share of the blame, a little less than his share of the credit.» - Arnold H. Glasow

#97 « A leader takes people where they would never go on their own.» - Hans Finzel

#98 « Leadership is one of sports' intangibles. Guys can score, guys can fight, guys can skate faster than anybody else. But not everybody can say, 'Follow me.'« - Paul Coffey

#99 « In 2015, 2016 before President Trump, there was a theme of hopelessness that good manufacturing jobs aren't coming back. Obama said you can't just wave a magic wand and bring these jobs back. Well, under President Trump and Amb. Lighthizer leadership on trade: Abracadabra!» - Bill Hagerty

#100 « Say what you will about the leadership of 'SNL,' they have crafted an institution as opposed to just running a show. I don't think that's by accident.» - Phil LaMarr

#101 « It's fair to characterise me as competitive and determined, but anyone who works with me will attest to the fact I believe very strongly in the notion of servant leadership.» - Irene Rosenfeld

#102 « If you spend your life trying to be good at everything, you will never be great at anything.» - Tom Rath

#103 « This assumption of Negro leadership in the ghetto, then, must not be confined to matters of religion, education, and social uplift; it must deal with such fundamental forces in life as make these things possible.» - Carter G. Woodson

#104 « Forget about the fast lane. If you really want to fly, just harness your power to your passion.» - Oprah Winfrey

#105 « The x» - factor of great leadership is not personality, it's humility. Jim Collins

#106 « The trouble with the Labour Party leadership and the trade union leadership, they're quite willing to applaud millions on the streets of the Philippines or in Eastern Europe, without understanding the need to also produce millions of people on the streets of Britain.» - Arthur Scargill

#107 « I think Mr. Clarke had a tendency to interfere too much with the activities of the CIA, and our leadership at the senior level let him interfere too much. So criticism from him I kind of wear as a badge of honor.» - Michael Scheuer

#108 « Leadership does not depend on being right.» - Ivan Illich

#109 « I think there is probably no better person to aspire to emulate than Steve Jobs and what he has done at Apple in terms of his leadership, his innovation, not settling for mediocrity.» - Howard Schultz

#110 « Leaders have to act more quickly today. The pressure comes much faster.» - Andy Grove

#111 « Comrade Deng Xiaoping - along with other party elders - gave the party leadership their firm and full support to put down the political disturbance using forceful measures.» - Li Peng

#112 « Leadership offers an opportunity to make a difference in someone's life, no matter what the project.» - Bill Owens

#113 « Leadership is unlocking people's potential to become better.» - Bill Bradley

#114 « The main tenet of design thinking is empathy for the people you're trying to design for. Leadership is exactly the same thing - building empathy for the people that you're entrusted to help.» - David M. Kelley

#115 « Leadership is intentional influence.» - Michael McKinney

#116 « I wish I had played team sports. I think every kid should. Teamwork builds character - teaches people about leadership and cooperation.» - Mo Rocca

#117 « The employer generally gets the employees he deserves.» - J. Paul Getty

#118 « Leadership is possible in all different ways, and in all different areas of life. Whether it is with friends or family, I expect them to set a great example for me, and hopefully I will do the same for them. And that is all part of being a leader.» - Steve Nash

#119 « This is the problem with the United States: there's no leadership. A leader would say, 'Police brutality is an oxymoron. There are no brutal police. The minute you become brutal you're no longer police.' So, what, we're not dealing with police. We're dealing with a federally authorized gang.» - KRS-One

#120 « There is a science to managing high tech businesses, and it needs to be respected. One of them is that in technology businesses, leadership is temporary. It's constantly recycling. So the asset has limited lifetime.» - Eric Schmidt

#121 « Don't follow the crowd, let the crowd follow you.» - Margaret Thatcher

#122 « Don't find fault, find a remedy.» - Henry Ford

#123 « Be kind, for everyone you meet is fighting a hard battle.» - Plato

#124 « President Roosevelt's leadership put the world on notice that the United States of America - with the freest, most dynamic economy the world had ever seen - was open for business.» - John Hoeven

#125 « A good objective of leadership is to help those who are doing poorly to do well and to help those who are doing well to do even better.» - Jim Rohn

#126 « I'm all for ambition and stretch goals. I set them for myself. But leadership isn't the same as cheerleading. Believing in something is a necessary but absolutely insufficient condition for making it come true.» - Margaret Heffernan

#127 « If one is lucky, a solitary fantasy can totally transform one million realities.» - Maya Angelou

#128 « Leadership and management are not synonymous.» - Travis Bradberry

#129 « A person always doing his or her best becomes a natural leader, just by example.» - Joe DiMaggio

#130 « Leadership is all about emotional intelligence. Management is taught, while leadership is experienced.» - Rajeev Suri

#131 « Strong convictions precede great actions.» - James Freeman Clarke

#132 « The only safe ship in a storm is leadership.» - Faye Wattleton

#133 « The Chinese leadership hoped that the world would soon forget the Tiananmen Square massacre. Our job in Congress is to ensure that we never forget those who lost their lives in Tiananmen Square that day or the pro-democracy cause for which they fought.» - Tom Lantos

#134 « Through the inspiration of Vaclav's words, the courage of his dissidence and the integrity of his leadership, Czechoslovakia successfully transitioned from an authoritarian state to a free democracy at the heart of Europe.» - Michael D. Higgins

#135 « Leading people is the most challenging and, therefore, the most gratifying undertaking of all human endeavors.» - Jocko Willink

#136 « There's the assumption being made by the national security advisers to the Obama administration that the North Korean leadership is not suicidal, that they know they will be obliterated if they attacked the United States. But I would point that everything in South Korea and Japan is well within range of what they might want to do.» - Oliver North

#137 « No organization should be allowed near disaster unless they are willing to cooperate with some level of established leadership.» - Irwin Redlener

#138 « I don't think leadership demands 'yes' or 'no' answers; I think leadership is providing the forum for making the right decision, which doesn't demand unanimity.» - Arthur Ochs Sulzberger, Jr.

#139 « People respond well to those that are sure of what they want.» - Anna Wintour

#140 « As we look ahead into the next century, leaders will be those who empower others» - Bill Gates

#141 « Leadership is intangible, and therefore no weapon ever designed can replace it.» - Omar N. Bradley

#142 « A man's doubts and fears are his worst enemy.» - William Wrigley, Jr.

#143 « I think to be a great quarterback, you have to have a great leadership, great attention to detail, and a relentless competitive nature. And that's what I try to bring to the table, and I have a long way to go. I'm still learning, and I'm still on a constant quest for knowledge.» - Russell Wilson

#144 « 'Always keep your eyes open. Keep watching. Because whatever you see can inspire you.'» - Grace Coddington

#145 « The longer we go without strong leadership from the Administration and until we see significant progress in the day-to-day lives of the Iraqi people, the more difficult it will become to sustain the support of the American people and Congress for the current course.» - Dennis Cardoza

#146 « I think in any situation, so much of effective leadership is when it comes from your own personality. And I feel very fortunate to be comfortable in the Colts locker room, where people can be who they are, and they don't have to change it when they show up to work that day.» - Andrew Luck

#147 « All of the great leaders have had one characteristic in common: it was the willingness to confront unequivocally the major anxiety of their people in their time. This, and not much else, is the essence of leadership.» - John Kenneth Galbraith

#148 « What helps people, helps business.» - Leo Burnett

#149 « Rotary provides training at all levels so that those who have been selected for leadership positions have the opportunity to learn and apply leadership principles to their jobs.» - Ron D. Burton

#150 « The intersection of political analysis and Internet theory is a busy crossroad of cliche, where familiar rhetorical vehicles - decentralized authority, emergent leadership, empowered grass roots - create a ceaseless buzz.» - Gary Wolf

#151 « Being a CEO still means sitting across the table from big institutional investors and showing your leadership and having them believe in you.» - Christie Hefner

#152 « Don't find fault, find a remedy.» - Henry Ford

#153 « You do not lead by hitting people over the head» - that's assault, not leadership. Dwight D. Eisenhower

#154 « Become the kind of leader that people would follow voluntarily; even if you had no title or position.» - Brian Tracy

#155 « Leadership is service to others.» - Denise Morrison

#156 « I believe in servant leadership, and the servant always asks, 'Where am I needed most?'« - Mike Pence

#157 « I think as far as any kind of pressure on a football team or on an individual in professional sports really depends not only on that individual but the leadership they have on the team and the leadership they have on the coaching staff. A lot of times, they can divert some of those pressures off of the individual and off of the team.» - Jimmy Johnson

#158 « A teacher affects eternity; he can never tell where his influence stops.» - Henry Adams

#159 « No man will make a great leader who wants to do it all himself or get all the credit for doing it.» - Andrew Carnegie

#160 « Putin's Russia is our adversary and moral opposite. It is committed to the destruction of the post-war, rule-based world order built on American leadership and the primacy of our political and economic values.» - John McCain

#161 « It is during our darkest moments that we must focus to see the light.» - Aristotle

#162 « To lead people, walk behind them.» - Lao Tzu

#163 « Leadership is hard to train on.» - Ben Horowitz

#164 « Man does not simply exist, but always decides what his existence will be, what he will become in the next moment.» - Viktor Frankl

#165 « I am often asked about the difference between 'change management' and 'change leadership,' and whether it's just a matter of semantics. These terms are not interchangeable.» - John P. Kotter

#166 « You just can't beat the person who never gives up.» - Babe Ruth

#167 « Sport fosters many things that are good; teamwork and leadership.» - Daley Thompson

#168 « Leadership is influence.» - John C. Maxwell

#169 « I think that in any group activity - whether it be business, sports, or family - there has to be leadership or it won't be successful.» - John Wooden

#170 « The sharp employ the sharp.» - Douglas William Jerrold

#171 « Stay focused, go after your dreams and keep moving toward your goals.» - LL Cool J

#172 « Europe is difficult to coordinate, and our main deficit may not even lie in this area of finance and economics, but in foreign and security policy. We have a leadership problem because we are still 27 different members who have still not decided on how to work with each other based on what we used to call a European constitution.» - Peer Steinbruck

#173 « I've been the co-chair of the Non-Partisan Women's Caucus and vice-chair for several years, taking a leadership role in this women's organization.» - Gwen Moore

#174 « Great leaders are not defined by the absence of weakness, but rather by the presence of clear strengths.» - John Zenger

#175 « Leadership is the art of accomplishing more than the science of management says is possible.» - Colin Powell

#176 « There is a real magic in enthusiasm. It spells the difference between mediocrity and accomplishment.» - Norman Vincent Peale

#177 « I don't want yes» - men around me. I want everyone to tell the truth, even if it costs them their jobs. - Samuel Goldwyn

#178 « No one is going to make you a leader. Take the reins, create your own opportunity, and build the career that you deserve.» - Devin Bramhall

#179 « It is a terrible thing to look over your shoulder when you are trying to lead» - and find no one there. - Franklin D. Roosevelt

#180 « We need leadership in this country, which will improve the lives of working families, the children, the elderly, the sick and the poor. We need leadership which brings our people together and makes us stronger.» - Bernie Sanders

#181 « In this nation, leadership is dollars.» - Norman Lear

#182 « Let the elders who rule well be considered worthy of double honor, especially those who labor in preaching and teaching.» - 1 Timothy 5:17

#183 « M&A at Microsoft is a team sport for the senior leadership group. They're all involved in it, and we all play different roles. My role is the first centralized business development role at Microsoft.» - Peggy Johnson

#184 « There is no finish line to leadership.» - Julia Hartz

#185 « Well, I've ruffled a few feathers at all the institutions I've led. But I think that's part of leadership.» - Robert M. Gates

#186 « Leadership is not about you; it's about investing in the growth of others.» - Ken Blanchard

#187 « Fall seven times and stand up eight.» - Japanese Proverb

#188 « My best successes came on the heels of failures.» - Barbara Corcoran

#189 « I think that's what's thrilling about leadership - when you're holding onto literally the worst possible hand on the planet and you know you're still going to win. How are you still going to win? Because that's when the character of the company really comes out.» - Jensen Huang

#190 « A cowardly leader is the most dangerous of men.» - Stephen King

#191 « On March 12, 2004, acting attorney general James B. Comey and the Justice Department's top leadership reached the brink of resignation over electronic surveillance orders that they believed to be illegal.» - Barton Gellman

#192 « Life is 10 percent what happens to me and 90 percent of how I react to it.» - Charles Swindoll

#193 « Leadership appears to be the art of getting others to want to do something you are convinced should be done.» - Vance Packard

#194 « A strong leader avoids becoming over» - confident to the point of impaired judgment. - Daniel Luetzky

#195 « If your actions inspire others to dream more, learn more, do more and become more, you are a leader.» - John Q. Adams

#196 « If people want to compete for leadership of a religious group, they can compete in piety. A chilling thought. Or funny.» - Mary Douglas

#197 « A goal properly set is halfway reached.» - Zig Ziglar

#198 « Leadership is about vision and responsibility, not power.» - Seth Berkley

#199 « Do unto others as you would have them do unto you.» - Jesus Christ

#200 « Power should be reserved for weightlifting and boats, and leadership really involves responsibility.» - Herb Kelleher

#201 « You don't get harmony when everybody sings the same note.» - Doug Floyd

#202 « For centuries, America has led the world on a long march toward freedom and democracy. Let's reclaim our clean energy leadership and lead the world toward clean energy independence.» - John Garamendi

#203 « Leadership is an ever-evolving position.» - Mike Krzyzewski

#204 « Helping other people develops your leadership skills, and people start to see you as a natural leader.» - Doug McMillon

#205 « I supported my friend Congressman Shuler over former Speaker Nancy Pelosi during our party's leadership elections in November citing a need for new leadership.» - Joe Donnelly

#206 « Leadership is, among other things, the ability to inflict pain and get away with it - short-term pain for long-term gain.» - George Will

#207 « The conduct of President Bush's war of choice has been plagued with incompetent civilian leadership decisions that have cost many lives and rendered the war on and occupation of Iraq a strategic policy disaster for the United States.» - John Olver

#208 « Leadership is... to make sure you never limit the idea or opportunity.» - Kevin Plank

#209 « The world is starving for original and decisive leadership.» - Bryant H. McGill

#210 « To succeed in business it is necessary to make others see things as you see them.» - Aristotle Onassis

#211 « To me, leadership is about encouraging people. It's about stimulating them. It's about enabling them to achieve what they can achieve - and to do that with a purpose.» - Christine Lagarde

#212 « You look at the quality players and look at the leadership we had, and it's easy to understand why we won.» - Bart Starr

#213 « The secret to success is good leadership, and good leadership is all about making the lives of your team members or workers better.» - Tony Dungy

#214 « Just as discipline and freedom are opposing forces that must be balanced, leadership requires finding the equilibrium in the dichotomy of many seemingly contradictory qualities between one extreme and another.» - Jocko Willink

#215 « You have to have your heart in the business and the business in your heart.» - An Wang

#216 « A genuine leader is not a searcher for consensus but a molder of consensus.» - Martin Luther King, Jr.

#217 « Presidential leadership needn't always cost money. Look for low- and no-cost options. They can be surprisingly effective.» - Donald Rumsfeld

#218 « When poor people get involved in a long conflict, such as a strike or a civil rights drive, and the pressure increases each day, there is a deep need for spiritual advice. Without it, we see families crumble, leadership weaken, and hard workers grow tired.» - Cesar Chavez

#219 « All of this suggests that while citizens became more comfortable with President Bush after

September 11 and thought him to have the requisite leadership skills, they continue to harbor doubts about his priorities, loyalties, interests, and policies.» - Thomas E. Mann

#220 « Real leaders must be ready to sacrifice all for the freedom of their people.» - Nelson Mandela

#221 « It is with obedience to your call that I take up the burden of government leadership for the final time.» - Kamisese Mara

#222 « There's two parts of leadership. You've got to be a good leader - you've got to be somebody that people want to emulate and care about the other people. But the other guys that you have have to accept their leadership. They have to respond to it. That's the chemistry that you never know how that is going to happen.» - Nick Saban

#223 « Among my activities was membership in the Boy Scouts; I rose each year through the ranks, eventually achieving the rank of Eagle Scout and undertaking leadership roles in the organization.» - Frederick Reines

#224 « Look for your choices, pick the best one, and then go for it!» - Pat Riley

#225 « If we will be quiet and ready enough, we shall find compensation in every disappointment.» - Henry David Thoreau

#226 « If you can provide the funding and you get the leadership, you'll have a competitive team.» - T. Boone Pickens

#227 « The world is fortunate - for the time being, at least - that it has an American president in Obama who is prepared to take a conciliatory and concessive attitude towards America's decline and that it has a Chinese leadership which has been extremely cautious about expressing an opinion, let alone flexing its muscles.» - Martin Jacques

#228 « The most common way people give up their power is by thinking they don't have any.» - Alice Walker

#229 « Humility is a great quality of leadership which derives respect and not just fear or hatred.» - Yousef Munayyer

#230 « The best thing you can do is learn from those mistakes so that you continue to get better. That's the management style or leadership style I believe in, which is push people to their limit such th
become better than they thought they cou
certainly has helped me.» - Lisa Su

#231 « A leader is one who sees more than others see, who sees farther than others see, and who sees before others see.» - Leroy Eimes

#232 « In fact, the converse is true: At a time when the United States has been called on for a level of moral leadership, vision and inspiration not seen since World War II, we cannot afford to dissemble about crimes against humanity.» - Adam Schiff

#233 « Leadership does matter.» - Mark Rutte

#234 « I think leadership is not something you learn; it's something you discover.» - Myles Munroe

#235 « To be elected president, you have to do more than tear down your opponents. You have to give the American people a reason to vote for you - a reason to hope - a reason to believe that under your leadership, America will be better.» - Mike DeWine

#236 « Real leadership is leaders recognising that they serve the people that they lead.» - Pete Hoekstra

#237 « A functioning, robust democracy requires a healthy educated, participatory followership, and an educated, morally grounded leadership.» - Chinua Achebe

#238 « A company is stronger if it is bound by love rather than by fear.» - Herb Kelleher

#239 « Leadership is loud. It is quiet. It is thoughtful and emotional and cerebral and nerdy and goofy and joyful and motivating.» - Julie Foudy

#240 « In working with UNICEF our corporate partners have demonstrated time and again that their financial resources, leadership and expertise can bring about real and lasting benefits for the world's children.» - Carol Bellamy

#241 « Leadership is something I was born with.» - Carmelo Anthony

#242 « One thing we've talked a lot about, even in the first leadership meeting, was, what's the purpose of our leadership team? The framework we came up with is the notion that our purpose is to bring clarity, alignment and intensity.» - Satya Nadella

#243 « We should see the leadership from the White House setting dates certain for certain goals of achieving greater alliance on alternative and renewable energy sources, but we are not.» - Ron Kind

#244 « How we think shows through in how we act. Attitudes are mirrors of the mind. They reflect thinking.» - David Joseph Schwartz

#245 « I think that all areas of the budget have to be scrubbed. Clearly the entitlement issues have to be reformed and that's an issue that's going to require I think some strong bipartisan cooperation and leadership.» - John Thune

#246 « As a woman, my style defines my leadership. It's a gentler, more compassionate approach. I consult, I listen and I compromise where it's in the best interest of the citizens.» - Kamla Persad-Bissessar

#247 « The sharp employ the sharp.» - Douglas William Jerrold

#248 « A good leader takes a little more than his share of the blame, a little less than his share of the credit.» - Arnold H. Glasow

#249 « The intelligence investigation under the leadership of Senator Church, which I know has helped cause this investigation by you, points out that the agencies did not disclose certain facts to us and that certain plots were going on.» - John Sherman Cooper

#250 « Don't tell people how to do things. Tell them what to do and let them surprise you with their results.» - George S. Patton Jr.

#251 « I think there are lots of ways to exercise ambition and accomplish things using leadership without going into elected politics. So, categorically, I have no intention of going into elected politics. None.» - Chris Hadfield

#252 « Example is leadership.» - Albert Schweitzer

#253 « I don't know any other way to lead but by example.» - Don Shula

#254 « Lead me, follow me, or get out of my way.» - General George Patton

#255 « President Ford was a devoted, decent man of impeccable integrity who put service to his country before his own self interest. He helped heal our nation during a time of crisis, provided steady leadership and restored people's faith in the presidency and in government.» - Mark Udall

#256 « Not all readers are leaders, but all leaders are readers.» - Harry S. Truman

#257 « I liked the military life. They teach you self-sufficiency early on. I always say that I learned most of what I know about leadership in the Marine Corps. Certain basic principles stay with you - sometimes consciously, mostly unconsciously.» - Raymond Kelly

#258 « Half a world away nations that once lived under oppression and tyranny are now budding democracies due in large part to America 's leadership and the sacrifices of our military.» - Bob Riley

#259 « We'll have a sales leader go run engineering. A lawyer go run business development. A business development leader go run our consumer operations. We're going to train a generalist group of leaders who know how to learn and operate in collaboration teamwork. I think that's the future of leadership.» - John T. Chambers

#260 « I'd like to believe that achieving a leadership position is all about competency, capability and ambition, so I try not to distinguish between the sexes when it comes to giving career advice.» - Heather Bresch

#261 « We can't drive our SUVs and eat as much as we want and keep our homes on 72 degrees at all times... and then just expect that other countries are going to say OK. That's not leadership. That's not going to happen.» - Barack Obama

#262 « Success is the progressive realization of a worthy goal or ideal.» - Earl Nightingale

#263 « If your situation» - be it your family, your team, your church, or your friends

#264 « The test of leadership for David Cameron was actually to bring the British Conservative Party back in to the mainstream.» - David Miliband

#265 « It is better to have a lion at the head of an army of sheep, than a sheep at the head of an army of lions.» - Daniel Defoe

#266 « Women account for about 70% of Africa's food production and manage a large proportion of small enterprises. They are also increasingly represented in legislative and executive leadership positions.» - Ngozi Okonjo-Iweala

#267 « I learned that leadership is about falling in love with the people and the people falling in love with you. It is about serving the people with selflessness, with sacrifice, and with the need to put the common good ahead of personal interests.» - Joyce Banda

#268 « Leadership is an opportunity to serve. It is not a trumpet call to self-importance.» - J. Donald Walters

#269 « A great person attracts great people and knows how to hold them together.» - Johann Wolfgang von Goethe

#270 « A man is only a leader when a follower stands beside him.» - Mark Brouwer

#271 « The great gift of human beings is that we have the power of empathy.» - Meryl Streep

#272 « I speak directly to the people, and I know that the people of California want to have better leadership. They want to have great leadership. They want to have somebody that will represent them. And it doesn't matter if you're a Democrat or a Republican, young or old.» - Arnold Schwarzenegger

#273 « As a woman leader, I thought I brought a different kind of leadership. I was interested in women's issues, in bringing down the population growth rate... as a woman, I entered politics with an additional dimension - that of a mother.» - Benazir Bhutto

#274 « The first responsibility of a leader is to define reality. The last is to say thank you. In between, the leader is a servant.» - Max DePree

#275 « Leadership is happening, but it's not coming from the leaders of the old institutions. Everywhere you look, you see these extraordinary, sparkling new initiatives that are under way.» - Don Tapscott

#276 « Stubbornness is a positive quality of presidential leadership - if you're right about what you're stubborn about.» - Douglas Brinkley

#277 « Leadership is about vision and responsibility, not power.» - Seth Berkley

#278 « By giving the leadership to the private sector in a capitalistic society, we're going to measure the value of art by how many products we can sell.» - Robert Wilson

#279 « Start where you are. Use what you have. Do what you can.» - Arthur Ashe

#280 « There was great leadership in this country at the time of World War II. There was also unrelenting resolve at home, in America's factories and on the farms, in the cities and the country.» - Bob Feller

#281 « We can't entrepreneur our way around bad leadership. We can't entrepreneur our way around bad policies. Those of us who have managed to entrepreneur ourselves out of it are living in a very false security in Africa.» - Ory Okolloh

#282 « What we achieve inwardly will change outer reality.» - Plutarch

#283 « 'It does not matter how slowly you go as long as you do not stop.'» - Confucius

#284 « Whether we're talking about leadership, teamwork, or client service, there is no more powerful attribute than the ability to be genuinely honest about one's weaknesses, mistakes, and needs for help.» - Patrick Lencioni

#285 « A boss says, Go! A leader says, Let's go!» - E.M. Kelly

#286 « Leadership is not about the next election, it's about the next generation.» - Simon Sinek

#287 « I think our leadership team is a highly accountable leadership team.» - Steve Ballmer

#288 « As far as my leadership style is concerned what makes me happiest is fulfilling my potential and helping others realize theirs. If you have really done that then the rest of it is actually very simple.» - Ashok Soota

#289 « I never dreamed about success. I worked for it.» - Estée Lauder

#290 « It's not easy for an entrepreneur to find the time to blog. But for those who do it, it is a great tool to communicate with the various stakeholders in their business and build a reputation for thought leadership.» - Fred Wilson

#291 « That is what leadership is all about: staking your ground ahead of where opinion is and convincing people, not simply following the popular opinion of the moment.» - Doris Kearns Goodwin

#292 « The most significant barrier to female leadership is the actual lack of females in leadership. The best advice I can give to women is to go out and start something, ideally their own businesses. If you can't see a path for leadership within your own company, go blaze a trail of your own.» - Safra A. Catz

#293 « Leadership is action, not position.» - Donald H. McGannon

#294 « My role at Lockheed Martin puts me in contact with extraordinary leaders in many fields - from science and engineering to philanthropy and government. And since we also work closely with our nation's armed forces, we tend to reflect a lot on leadership and how we can inspire successful teamwork, cooperation, and partnerships.» - Marillyn Hewson

#295 « I can give you a six» - word formula for success: Think things through - Eddie Rickenbacker

#296 « Don't be selfish; don't try to impress others. Be humble, thinking of others as better than yourselves.» - Philippians 2:3

#297 « Leadership is action, not position.» - Donald H. McGannon

#298 « It is better to have one person working with you, than three working for you.» - Unknown

#299 « Benchmarking is an ongoing exercise in any company that aspires for leadership.» - Anand Mahindra

#300 « I fell in love with the topic of leadership. For three decades, that has been a major focus of my hands-on work: listening to and working with leaders, their teams and their organizations.» - Henry Cloud

#301 « Leadership offers an opportunity to make a difference in someone's life, no matter what the project.» - Bill Owens

#302 « But I think Steve's main contribution besides just the pure leadership is his passion for excellence. He's a perfectionist. Good enough isn't good enough. And also his creative spirit. You know he really, really wants to do something great.» - Andy Hertzfeld

#303 « Getting in touch with your true self must be your first priority.» - Tom Hopkins

#304 « Leadership is not about a title or a designation. It's about impact, influence, and inspiration.» - Robin S. Sharma

#305 « One must be convinced to convince, to have enthusiasm to stimulate the others.» - Stefan Zweig

#306 « Moreover, as the leadership of the House confirmed last year, the Administration remains opposed to a congressional resolution on the Armenian Genocide due to Turkish objections. This approach sends absolutely the wrong signal to Turkey and to the rest of the world.» - Patrick J. Kennedy

#307 « Research shows that girls look at leadership differently than boys.» - Anna Maria Chavez

#308 « I am not in favour of quotas. Just put the best person into the job. It is not about gender; it is about experience, leadership and vision.» - Angela Ahrendts

#309 « A leader is a dealer in hope.» - Napoleon

#310 « Leadership is practiced not so much in words as in attitude and in actions.» - Harold S. Geneen

#311 « My senior leadership team is half people who have been at GM for a long period of time like me, and others who have joined the company within the last five years from different industries, experiences, and countries. You have a better picture of the world. The diversity of thought is where you can make better business decisions.» - Mary Barra

#312 « The cardinal responsibility of leadership is to identify the dominant contradiction at each point of the historical process and to work out a central line to resolve it.» - Mao Zedong

#313 « Leadership is hard to define and good leadership even harder. But if you can get people to follow you to the ends of the earth, you are a great leader.» - Indra Nooyi

#314 « Yahoo! is the only company with both scale and leadership in branded and search advertising.» - Terry Semel

#315 « Sometimes leadership is planting trees under whose shade you'll never sit. It may not happen fully till after I'm gone. But I know that the steps we're taking are the right steps.» - Jennifer Granholm

#316 « In politics, as in business, leadership is crucial.» - Edgar Bronfman, Sr.

#317 « You cannot transpose the U.S. system on Turkey, and the Turkish system on France etc. You have to understand the people and their culture. That's leadership.» - Hamad bin Isa Al Khalifa

#318 « Leadership must be likeable, affable, cordial, and above all emotional. The fashion of authoritarian leadership is gone. Football is about life. You can't be angry all day.» - Vicente del Bosque

#319 « I think for leadership positions, emotional intelligence is more important than cognitive intelligence. People with emotional intelligence usually have a lot of cognitive intelligence, but that's not always true the other way around.» - John Mackey

#320 « Charter laws do something really important. They give educators the freedom and flexibility that they need to attain results. But we also have to invest a lot in the leadership pipeline to take advantage of that freedom and flexibility.» - Wendy Kopp

#321 « If you care enough for a result, you will most certainly attain it.» - William James

#322 « Leadership is absolutely about inspiring action, but it is also about guarding against mid» - action. - Simon Sinek

#323 « The war and terrorism in the Middle East, the crisis of leadership in many of the oil-supply countries in the developing world, the crisis of global warming - all these are very clearly tied to energy.» - Julia Louis-Dreyfus

#324 « If you want to improve the organization, you have to improve yourself and the organization gets pulled up with you.» - Indra Nooyi

#325 « With King Abdullah's leadership and his people's trust he can keep the kingdom stable and secure in all its affairs.» - Sultan bin Abdul-Aziz Al Saud

#326 « I always liked the idea of leadership and being a captain.» - Dylan Lauren

#327 « We need to make sure we're creating spaces to create new leaders and new types of leadership.» - Alicia Garza

#328 « We need leadership that can elevate religion and morality to their position of paramount importance and thus eliminate growing selfishness, immorality and materialism.» - George W. Romney

#329 « One simple way to keep organizations from becoming cancerous might be to rotate all jobs on a regular, frequent and mandatory basis, including the leadership positions.» - Robert Shea

#330 « Leadership is a choice, not a position.» - Stephen Covey

#331 « My job is not to be easy on people. My job is to take these great people we have and to push them and make them even better.» - Steve Jobs

#332 « The public sector certainly includes the Department of Labor. Those are jobs that are available. They are open and they are good paying jobs. The government as a whole has been actually retrenching under President Clinton's leadership.» - Alexis Herman

#333 « Leadership is neither about you or me; it is about something that needs to be done. Leaders figure out how it can be made to happen and get ten or a million people to see that this is the way to do it.» - Jaggi Vasudev

#334 « Leadership is diving for a loose ball, getting the crowd involved, getting other players involved. It's being able to take it as well as dish it out. That's the only way you're going to get respect from the players.» - Larry Bird

#335 « There are no ideas in the Republican Party right now in the Congress. They're the party of no. They desperately need some intellectual leadership. And whatever you think of Newt Gingrich, he can supply intellectual leadership. So I hope he does run.» - Howard Dean

#336 « The role of leadership is to transform the complex situation into small pieces and prioritize them.» - Carlos Ghosn

#337 « The United States is the most innovative country in the world. But our leadership could slip away if we fail to properly fund primary, secondary and higher education.» - Jeff Bingaman

#338 « The problem with being a leader is that you're never sure if you're being followed or chased.» - Claire A. Murray

#339 « I hope telling the story of how I went from being a single mom to serving in the Texas State Senate to running for governor will remind others that with the right leadership in government, where you start has nothing to do with how far you go.» - Wendy Davis

#340 « Governments follow their people. A great deal has to do with the vision of the leadership of governments. They have a vision, and they translate that to their people and to their counterparts in other countries. You can fulfill and achieve a great deal if you get along well as individuals, as people, as persons.» - Salman Khurshid

#341 « I would say that one of the things that encouraged me so much when I became elected to the leadership was the letters I received from fathers of daughters, saying that, 'My daughter can now do many more things because of what you did.'« - Nancy Pelosi

#342 « The tradition that I come from has a great influence on Karnataka. Not just politically - it's also my social and moral responsibility to draw citizens facing bad governance and lawlessness to a leadership that is capable of delivering good governance and development.» - Yogi Adityanath

#343 « The Vatican's recognition of the State of Israel in 1997 could not have occurred without John Paul's leadership.» - David Novak

#344 « Effective leadership is not about making speeches or being liked; leadership is defined by results not attributes.» - Peter Drucker

#345 « You can never cross the ocean until you have the courage to lose sight of the shore.» - Christopher Columbus

#346 « One thing that somebody told me is that leadership is a lonely role - some people can do it, and some people can't.» - Kyrie Irving

#347 « If you're running an engineering or finance company, all companies depend on ideas and ingenuity. I think the principles of creative leadership apply everywhere, whether it's an advertising company or whether you're running a hospital.» - Ken Robinson

#348 « For many members of Congress, the time for choosing is near - do what the party leadership demands, or do what the people have asked you to do. If my colleagues don't mind some advice from a newcomer, I'd suggest going with the will of the people.» - Scott Brown

#349 « Everyone who's ever taken a shower has an idea. It's the person who gets out of the shower, dries off and does something about it who makes a difference.» - Nolan Bushnell

#350 « Leadership and learning are indispensable to each other.» - John F. Kennedy

#351 « It's a tremendous responsibility to be direct descendants of the prophet Muhammad. This family has had the burden of leadership on its shoulders for

1,400 years. I'm not going to drop the ball on my shift.» - Abdullah II of Jordan

#352 « Scott Walker has provided some really excellent leadership in Wisconsin.» - Ron Johnson

#353 « It takes a great man to be a good listener.» - Calvin Coolidge

#354 « The things journalists should pay attention to are the issues the political leadership agrees on, rather than to their supposed antagonisms.» - Michael Pollan

#355 « There is nothing that Bitcoin can do which Ethereum can't. While Ethereum is less battle-tested, it is moving faster, has better leadership, and has more developer mindshare.» - Fred Ehrsam

#356 « The successful warrior is the average man, with laserlike focus.» - Bruce Lee

#357 « In teamwork, silence isn’t golden. It’s deadly.» - Mark Sanborn

#358 « It simply cannot be disputed that for decades the Palestinian leadership was more interested in there not being a Jewish state than in there being a Palestinian state.» - Alan Dershowitz

#359 « Instead of begging OPEC to drop its oil prices, let's use American leadership and ingenuity to solve our own energy problems.» - Pete Domenici

#360 « In giving us children, God places us in a position of both leadership and service. He calls us to give up our lives for someone else's sake - to abandon our own desires and put our child's interests first. Yet, according to His perfect design, it is through this selflessness that we can become truly fulfilled.» - Charles Stanley

#361 « Leadership is not a basket of tricks or strategies or skills that you pull out. Leadership begins with the quality of the person.» - Frances Hesselbein

#362 « If you want to build something great, you should focus on what the change is that you want to make in the world.» - Mark Zuckerberg

#363 « If we are to negotiate the coming years safely, we may need a new kind of leadership. To put it more precisely, we need the rediscovery of an ancient kind of leadership that has rarely been given the prominence it deserves. I mean the leader as teacher.» - Jonathan Sacks

#364 « A leader does not deserve the name unless he is willing occasionally to stand alone.» - Henry Kissinger

#365 « I knew I could not maintain that leadership in open struggle against Moscow influence. Only two Communist leaders in history ever succeeded in doing this - Tito and Mao Tse-tung.» - Earl Browder

#366 « We need leadership, and we need it now.» - Byron Dorgan

#367 « Let us build a 21st-century rural economy of cutting-edge companies and technologies that lead us to energy and food security. Such an investment will revitalize rural America, re-establish our moral leadership on climate security and eliminate our addiction to foreign oil.» - Tom Vilsack

#368 « I never get bored talking about themes dealing with ambition, leadership and what it means to be an American. I love that stuff. I just love it. I've loved it ever since I was on 'The West Wing.'« - Rob Lowe

#369 « The greatest gift of leadership is a boss who wants you to be successful.» - Jon Taffer

#370 « The hardest thing in leadership is managing your own psychology, and yet it's also the least talked about.» - Andy Dunn

#371 « Leadership is the art of giving people a platform for spreading ideas that work.» - Seth Godin

#372 « Divorced from ethics, leadership is reduced to management and politics to mere technique.» - James MacGregor Burns

#373 « You have enemies? Good. That means you've stood up for something, sometime in your life.» - Winston Churchill

#374 « The highest of distinctions is service to others.» - King George VI

#375 « Don't tell people how to do things, tell them what to do and let them surprise you with their results.» - George Patton

#376 « When people are placed in positions slightly above what they expect, they are apt to excel.» - Richard Branson

#377 « If you want to get the most out of your men, give them a break! Don't make them work completely in the dark. If you do, they won't do a bit more than they have to. But if they comprehend, they'll work like mad.» - Chesty Puller

#378 « Leaders grasp nettles.» - David Ogilvy

#379 « The very essence of leadership is that you have to have vision. You can't blow an uncertain trumpet.» - Theodore M. Hesburgh

#380 « Management is about arranging and telling. Leadership is about nurturing and enhancing.» - Tom Peters

#381 « Education is the mother of leadership» - Wendell Willkie

#382 « Leadership is simply the ability of an individual to coalesce the efforts of other individuals toward achieving common goals. It boils down to looking after your people and ensuring that, from top to bottom, everyone feels part of the team.» - Frederick W. Smith

#383 « Leadership is about making others better as a result of your presence and making sure that impact lasts in your absence.» - Sheryl Sanberg

#384 « Real leaders are ordinary people with extraordinary determinations.» - John Seaman Garns

#385 « Clarity affords focus.» - Thomas Leonard

#386 « Indeed, there is an eloquence in true enthusiasm that is not to be doubted.» - Edgar Allan Poe

#387 « The failure of women to have reached positions of leadership has been due in large part to social and professional discrimination. In the past, few women have tried, and even fewer have succeeded.» - Rosalyn Sussman Yalow

#388 « If America wants to retain its position as a global power, its president must listen to the people and show strong leadership at this turning point in human history.» - David Suzuki

#389 « To do great things is difficult; but to command great things is more difficult.» - Friedrich Nietzsche

#390 « I think Chinese leadership is trying to tell the world they have another set of logic or reasoning or values which are different from yours. Of course, I don't think they believe that. It's just an argument that's made when you can't confront the truth and facts. They really want to maintain power.» - Ai Weiwei

#391 « You can’t fake listening. It shows.» - Raquel Welch

#392 « The greatest leaders mobilize others by coalescing people around a shared vision.» - Ken Blanchard

#393 « I want American Dream growth - lots of new businesses, well-paying jobs, and American leadership in new industries, like clean energy and biotechnology.» - William J. Clinton

#394 « Leadership is more about clarity than it is about control.» - Mark Goulston

#395 « There is usually an 'X factor' that is hard to define. For HTC, I think it is our culture. We embrace the best of our Eastern roots and combine it with the best of the Western cultures where we have leadership and offices. It makes the culture colorful as well as energetic and creative.» - Cher Wang

#396 « The speed of the leader is the speed of the gang.» - Mary Kay Ash

#397 « I am not afraid of an army of lions led by a sheep; I am afraid of an army of sheep led by a lion.» - Alexander the Great

#398 « Example is not the main thing in influencing others. It is the only thing.» - Albert Schweitzer

#399 « Individual and corporate support is vital to building on London's leadership in the arts, and I hope others will join me in wanting to build on the National's role at the heart of modern theatre and sustaining it long into the future.» - Lloyd Dorfman

#400 « I've always voted Republican because America is exactly that, a republic. You can't expect much leadership with a Democrat behind the desk their not even close to dual efficient.» - Audrey Meadows

#401 « I've always been about the power of a woman - accentuating the positive, deleting the negative, whether you're talking her body, her voice or her leadership.» - Donna Karan

#402 « At the heart of great leadership is a curious mind, heart, and spirit.» - Chip Conley

#403 « I feel fantastically excited that we have a leader who fought for the leadership without compromising his quite challenging view that the party has to change.» - Francis Maude

#404 « I look for what needs to be done. After all, that's how the universe designs itself.» - R. Buckminster Fuller

#405 « Leadership has a harder job to do than just choose sides. It must bring sides together.» - Jesse Jackson

#406 « The king establishes the land by justice, But he who receives bribes overthrows it.» - Proverbs 29:4

#407 « If you tell the truth, you don't have to remember anything.» - Mark Twain

#408 « Only one man in a thousand is a leader of men» - the other 999 follow women. Groucho Marx

#409 « When the righteous increase, the people rejoice, But when a wicked man rules, people groan.» - Proverbs 29:2

#410 « I am a general. My soldiers are the keys and I have to command them.» - Vladimir Horowitz

#411 « When we see a lack of leadership coming from the White House, that's what brings leaders in Turkey to attack Israel the way they do. When we see a lack of leadership coming from the White House, that's why we see the leader of Iran... continuing to build the nuclear reactors.» - Danny Danon

#412 « IBM has taken a leadership role in this area and is prepared to be a technology partner with companies around the world to take advantage of these new developments.» - John Patrick

#413 « Certain things catch your eye, but pursue only those that capture the heart.» - Ancient Indian Proverb

#414 « Either you run the day, or the day runs you.» - Jim Rohn

#415 « I had the closest thing I have ever had to an out-of-body experience lying in bed one morning. I turned on the 'Today' programme and item four on the news was: 'The shadow chancellor has ruled himself out of the leadership.' I lay there thinking that's interesting, then I realised it was me.» - George Osborne

#416 « In the future, there will be no female leaders. There will just be leaders.» - Sheryl Sandberg

#417 « There are some members of the House leadership whose only mission in life is to demonize the president.» - John Kennedy

#418 « Leadership to me means duty, honor, country. It means character, and it means listening from time to time.» - George W. Bush

#419 « Alliances and international organizations should be understood as opportunities for leadership and a means to expand our influence, not as constraints on our power.» - Chuck Hagel

#420 « A leader is admired, a boss is feared.» - Vicente Del Bosque

#421 « Market leadership can translate directly to higher revenue, higher profitability, greater capital velocity, and correspondingly stronger returns on invested capital.» - Jeff Bezos

#422 « The notion of 'world leadership' is a curiously archaic one. The very phrase is redolent of Kipling ballads and James Bondian adventures. What makes a country a world leader? Is it population, in which case India is on course to top the charts, overtaking China as the world's most populous country by 2034?» - Shashi Tharoor

#423 « Leadership means forming a team and working toward common objectives that are tied to time, metrics, and resources.» - Russel Honore

#424 « Germany must be a country which generates political ideas and leadership, which is capable of compromise, which is sovereign and yet knows that it needs its partners on both sides of the Atlantic.» - Horst Koehler

#425 « Nothing will work unless you do.» - Maya Angelou

#426 « It is essential to employ, trust, and reward those whose perspective, ability, and judgment are radically different from yours. It is also rare, for it requires uncommon humility, tolerance, and wisdom.» - Dee Hock

#427 « The task of the leader is to get his people from where they are to where they have not been.» - Henry A. Kissinger

#428 « There are racial and gender implications to how we think about what leadership looks like in the country.» - Stacey Abrams

#429 « Ray Lewis, I've grown up watching Ray Lewis. Just watching his intensity, his passion for the game, his love for the game, his work ethic. Everything in a linebacker that you want to be is in Ray Lewis, from leadership qualities, all that.» - Manti Te'o

#430 « There are three secrets to managing. The first secret is have patience. The second is be patient. And the third most important secret is patience.» - Chuck Tanner

#431 « A leader is a person you will follow to a place you would not go by yourself.» - Joel Barker

#432 « Don't follow the crowd, let the crowd follow you.» - Margaret Thatcher

#433 « One of my beliefs about leadership is it's not how many followers you have, but how many people you have with different opinions that you can bring together and try to be a good listener.» - Robert Kraft

#434 « Leadership is practiced not so much in words as in attitude and in actions.» - Harold S. Green

#435 « People who enjoy meetings should not be in charge of anything.» - Thomas Sowell

#436 « One of the things about leadership is that you've got to show up. And if you want to be president of the United States you've got to make a case to the American people that Barack Obama needs to be dismissed from his position.» - Tim Pawlenty

#437 « The supreme quality of leadership is integrity.» - Dwight D. Eisenhower

#438 « A leader is one who knows the way, goes the way, and shows the way.» - John Maxwell

#439 « Basketball Without Borders is a leadership camp that takes basketball to different places around the world, to Africa, Europe, America and Asia. It's a camp that brings players from different parts of the continent to one city that's been assigned as the host city. We've been going to a different city every year.» - Dikembe Mutombo

#440 « I think directors should be confident in their leadership capabilities. I think directors should be confident in what they want to do.» - Philip Seymour Hoffman

#441 « 'Every life is a story. Make yours a best» - seller.' - Reback

#442 « Character matters; leadership descends from character.» - Rush Limbaugh

#443 « My philosophy of leadership is to surround myself with good people who have ability, judgment and knowledge, but above all, a passion for service.» - Sonny Perdue

#444 « If a king judges the poor with truth, His throne will be established forever.» - Proverbs 29:14

#445 « I made a commitment... both to myself and to some supporters to carefully consider a run for the

Liberal leadership for the Liberal Party of Canada.» - Dalton McGuinty

#446 « The 9/11 Commission recently released their report, citing important changes which need to be made to improve our nation's homeland security. I voiced my disappointment with the House leadership when this report was left until after the August recess for action.» - Leonard Boswell

#447 « Real leadership means tackling tough problems ourselves and not leaving them to our children.» - Jon Kyl

#448 « Do what you feel in your heart to be right» - for you'll be criticised anyway. - Eleanor Roosevelt

#449 « Leadership does take work. And it should. If you aspire to be a leader, you ought to treat leadership as a craft, you ought to become a student of it, and you ought to work at it. And if you're not willing to work at it, well, you get what you give.» - Douglas Conant

#450 « I am deeply honored by the trust the board has placed in me to lead Duke Energy. I have a high degree of confidence in the strength of our company's leadership and dedicated employees.» - Lynn Good

#451 « I think leadership is service and there is power in that giving: to help people, to inspire and motivate them to reach their fullest potential.» - Denise Morrison

#452 « The world needs new leadership, but the new leadership is about working together.» - Jack Ma

#453 « We have to trust the voices of the community to be in leadership and know what we need for our communities.» - Tarana Burke

#454 « In any leadership position, you're always going to be disappointing somebody.» - Biz Stone

#455 « Effective leadership is putting first things first. Effective management is discipline, carrying it out.» - Stephen Covey

#456 « A genuine leader is not a searcher for consensus but a molder of consensus.» - Dr. Martin Luther King, Jr.

#457 « A man always has two reasons for doing anything: a good reason and the real reason.» - J. P. Morgan

#458 « Eighty percent of success is showing up.» - Woody Allen

#459 « It is an abomination for kings to commit wicked acts, For a throne is established on righteousness.» - Proverbs 16:12

#460 « Humility is a great quality of leadership which derives respect and not just fear or hatred.» - Yousef Munayyer

#461 « You get in life what you have the courage to ask for.» - Nancy D. Solomon

#462 « A good leader can't get too far ahead of his followers.» - Franklin D. Roosevelt

#463 « Why would I be willing to challenge my Republican leadership? Because my allegiance will always be to the Constitution and the American people first and foremost, not to my political party.» - Matt Salmon

#464 « He who postpones the hour of living is like the rustic who waits for the river to run out before he crosses.» - Horace

#465 « This Congress is simply not doing its job under Republican leadership.» - Jim Cooper

#466 « The world needs new leadership, but the new leadership is about working together.» - Jack Ma

#467 « Don't necessarily avoid sharp edges. Occasionally they are necessary to leadership.» - Donald Rumsfeld

#468 « You're short on ears and long on mouth.» - John Wayne

#469 « Leaders of the future will have to be visionary and be able to bring people in - real communicators. These are things that women bring to leadership and executive positions, and it's going to be incredibly valuable and incredibly in demand.» - Anita Borg

#470 « A fool vents all his feelings, But a wise man holds them back.» - Proverbs 29:11

#471 « Integrity, insight, and inclusiveness are the three essential qualities of leadership.» - Sadhguru

#472 « We hire military veterans because they make great employees. They bring proven technical and leadership skills. They understand teamwork, and they're adaptable. Bottom line, hiring veterans is good for business.» - Randall L. Stephenson

#473 « Sometimes leadership is planting trees under whose shade you'll never sit.» - Jennifer Granholm

#474 « In terms of personalities - I don't care about the personalities, I want leadership that's in favor of my principles: free markets, adherence to the Constitution, and equal treatment for everyone under the law.» - Dave Brat

#475 « Our world desperately needs real leadership.» - Daniel Lubetzky

#476 « We must accept finite disappointment, but never lose infinite hope.» - Martin Luther King Jr

#477 « Millions saw the apple fall, but Newton was the one who asked why.» - Bernard Baruch

#478 « My student days in PSG saw three Prime Ministers, two wars, taught us courage, resilience, leadership and optimism.» - Shiv Nadar

#479 « The first responsibility of a leader is to define reality.» - Max De Pree

#480 « When your values are clear to you, making decisions becomes easier.» - Roy E. Disney

#481 « In Illinois, where legislators are paid» 45,000, plus as much as» 10,000 for leadership work, about half are full-time politicians.» - Bill Dedman

#482 « Leadership and learning are indispensable to each other.» - John F. Kennedy

#483 « I want to see a player on the football field. I want to see what kind of teammate they are, what kind of leadership qualities they have. I want to see how aggressive they are, how much fun they have playing the game.» - Roy Clark

#484 « Leaders need to be optimists. Their vision is beyond the present.» - Rudy Giuliani

#485 « You watch television and see what's going on on this debt ceiling issue. And what I consider to be a total lack of leadership from the President and nothing's going to get fixed until the President himself steps up and wrangles both parties in Congress.» - Steve Wynn

#486 « Leadership is standing with your people. People say you have to live to fight another day, but sometimes you have to show you are a true leader.» - Leymah Gbowee

#487 « Leadership is unlocking people's potential to become better.» - Bill Bradley

#488 « Do not speak in the hearing of a fool, For he will despise the wisdom of your words.» - Proverbs 23:9

#489 « The one thing that the President can do is to establish a real energy independence plan. We have all the recources we need right here in this country to establish energy independence if we had the leadership.» - Herman Cain

#490 « Leadership is an opportunity to serve. It is not a trumpet call to self» - importance. - J. Donald Walters

#491 « Leadership is the other side of the coin of loneliness, and he who is a leader must always act alone. And acting alone, accept everything alone.» - Ferdinand Marcos

#492 « The atmosphere at my school was very competitive. Young girls were competing with each other every day for status, for leadership, for the affection of the teachers. I hated it.» - Zhang Ziyi

#493 « There is something discordant about a team of speechwriters and political operatives hammering away to create an image of the 'real, inner' candidate. And, to be blunt, there is no necessary connection between a moving life experience and the skills necessary for leadership.» - Jeff Greenfield

#494 « If you can dream it, you can do it.» - Walt Disney

#495 « A leader is someone who helps improve the lives of other people or improve the system they live under.» - Sam Houston

#496 « Don't judge each day by the harvest you reap but by the seeds that you plant.» - Robert Louis Stevenson

#497 « History has shown that one cannot legislate a culture of integrity. And yet, one of the paramount responsibilities and challenges of corporate leadership is to ensure such a culture.» - Preet Bharara

#498 « This is about systemic, institutional corruption, not personality. To ask the Democratic leadership to clean things up would be like asking the old Soviet bureaucracy under Brezhnev to reform itself. It ain't going to happen.» - Newt Gingrich

#499 « Across Africa there is what I call a colonialist mentality or orthodoxy. Orthodoxy in the sense that a lot of things have gone wrong in Africa in the post-colonial period. And time and time again, any time something went wrong, the leadership claims that it was never their fault.» - George Ayittey

#500 « Republicans working in leadership and the trenches are largely old, white, male, out-of-touch, out of ideas, technology averse, and living in the past.» - Mark McKinnon

#501 « Each year I host a leadership summit in my district, and my biggest advice to young people is get experience. Get your foot in the door.» - Aaron Schock

#502 « I've developed a huge regard for Toyota for its environmental awareness, for its immense commitment to research and development in this field, and for its leadership in developing hybrids which others are now following.» - Maurice Strong

#503 « Inspirational leaders need to have a winning mentality in order to inspire respect. It is hard to trust in the leadership of someone who is half-hearted about their purpose, or only sporadic in focus or enthusiasm.» - Sebastian Coe

#504 « Management is about arranging and telling. Leadership is about nurturing and enhancing.» - Tom Peters

#505 « Every time you have to speak, you are auditioning for leadership.» - James Humes

#506 « The school made it very clear that women were entitled to positions of authority. That sense of entitlement allowed us to feel that we have a natural place in leadership in the world. That gave me a mental and emotional confidence.» - Linda Vester

#507 « Life isn't easy, and leadership is harder still.» - Walter Russell Mead

#508 « When your work speaks for itself, don’t interrupt.» - Henry J. Kaiser

#509 « To handle yourself, use your head; to handle others, use your heart.» - Eleanor Roosevelt

#510 « We shouldn't be debating whether to deal with the current code by allowing it to be extended or not. We should have a president who shows leadership and comes to Congress and says: 'You know what? We need to reform this whole tax code.'« - Rob Portman

#511 « Overall, the challenge of leadership is both moral and one of developing the characteristics that make us respected by one another.» - Louis Farrakhan

#512 « Positive leadership - conveying the idea that there is always a way forward - is so important, because that is what you are here for - to figure out how to move the organization forward. Critical to doing that is reinforcing the idea that everyone is included.» - Alan Mulally

#513 « Leadership - mobilization toward a common goal.» - Garry Wills

#514 « To succeed in business it is necessary to make others see things as you see them.» - Aristotle Onassis

#515 « My mom was the first African-American woman to graduate from the University of Chicago Law School, in 1946. She had leadership roles in the law, in government and the corporate world. She was a great role model in that she felt anything was possible.» - John W. Rogers, Jr.

#516 « The more I'm pushed in a position of leadership and I know I have to be the mouthpiece for so many other people who can't speak for themselves, the more confidence I'm gaining.» - Viola Davis

#517 « Real leadership is leaders recognizing that they serve the people that they lead.» - Pete Hoekstra

#518 « Leadership is a privilege to better the lives of others. It is not an opportunity to satisfy personal greed.» - Mwai Kibaki

#519 « Leaders think and talk about the solutions. Followers think and talk about the problems.» - Brian Tracy

#520 « If you want a quality, act as if you already have it.» - William James

#521 « There are many elements to a campaign. Leadership is number one. Everything else is number two.» - Bertolt Brecht

#522 « If you want to make enemies, try to change something.» - Woodrow Wilson

#523 « Only one man in a thousand is a leader of men - the other 999 follow women. » - Groucho Marx

#524 « As we look ahead into the next century, leaders will be those who empower others.» - Bill Gates

#525 « I urge the Iraqi leadership for sake of its own people... to seize this opportunity and thereby begin to end the isolation and suffering of the Iraqi people.» - Kofi Annan

#526 « Different times need different types of leadership.» - Park Geun-hye

#527 « The more I have studied Lincoln, the more I have followed his thought processes, the more I am convinced that he understood leadership better than any other American president.» - David Herbert Donald

#528 « Leadership is one of the things I really strive to excel in in my life.» - Nate Parker

#529 « A lot of young people just starting out unskilled, as all Americans do when they're born here, come to this country, and so the business community is for immigration. Big businesses, small businesses, high-tech, low-tech, the communities of faith, and the Republican leadership.» - Grover Norquist

#530 « The only safe ship in a storm is leadership.» - Faye Wattleton

#531 « The first key to leadership is self» - control. - Jack Weatherford

#532 « Well, I think that» - I think leadership's always been about two main things: imagination and courage. - Paul Keating

#533 « Great leaders delegate and nurture future leaders.» - Invajy

#534 « The real leader has no need to lead» - he is content to point the way.

#535 « He also told them this parable: Can the blind lead the blind? Will they not both fall into a pit?» - Luke 6:39

#536 « Management is doing things right; leadership is doing the right thing.» - Peter F. Drucker

#537 « There's no doubt West Point impacted who I am... It has an enormous emphasis, not only on military aspects, but character development. Whether it's the honor code, or the interactions you have, both with the çadet leadership and the academy leadership, every place you are is a character test.» - Mike Pompeo

#538 « Too often, advances in civil rights or women's rights are undermined by wrong-headed legislation or weak-kneed political leadership.» - Mike Quigley

#539 « America somehow thinks that leadership relates to governance, and it certainly does. But society is much bigger than governance, and some of the truly great leadership of our society is outside the governance arena.» - Jim Leach

#540 « So I think democracy, in the long-term, in our countries will survive if it comes to be associated with leadership, will not survive if democracy plus media brings to us more and more followship rather than leadership.» - Mario Monti

#541 « I attended Florida State University on an academic and leadership scholarship, changed my major from biology to broadcasting, and transferred to the University of South Carolina for my last two years.» - Ainsley Earhardt

#542 « Ben Roethlisberger is a proven winner in athletic competition. But the measure of a true leader is how they conduct themselves 24/7, not just during a winning touchdown drive or a goal-line stance. Leadership isn't something that gets switched off because the game clock expires.» - Jackson Katz

#543 « Whatever the mind of man can conceive and believe, it can achieve.» - Napoleon Hill

#544 « You don't lead by hitting people over the head» - that's assault, not leadership. » - Dwight D. Eisenhower

#545 « I could always score goals. I loved that feeling of having your team look to you, that feeling of leadership.» - Alex Morgan

#546 « The topic of leadership is a touchy one. A lot of leaders fail because they don't have the bravery to touch that nerve or strike that chord. Throughout my years, I haven't had that fear.» - Kobe Bryant

#547 « The Dalai Lama. He is a very wise man of great inner peace who believes that happiness is the purpose of our lives. Through his teachings and leadership, he continues to make this world a better place in which to live.» - Sidney Sheldon

#548 « If you have ideas, you have the main asset you need, and there isn't any limit to what you can do with your business and your life. Ideas are any man's greatest asset.» - Harvey S. Firestone

#549 « If the highest aim of a captain were to preserve his ship, he would keep it in port forever.» - Thomas Aquinas

#550 « We have now under President Obama's leadership had 29 months in a row of private sector job growth. That stretch of positive private sector job growth hasn't happened since 2005. We still have a long way to go, but we are moving in the right direction.» - Martin O'Malley

#551 « As for leadership, I am the kind who leads reluctantly and more by example than anything else. Someone had to be on the incorporation papers as president.» - Keith Henson

#552 « Enthusiasm is a vital element toward the individual success of every man or woman.» - Conrad Hilton

#553 « .....from everyone who has been given much shall much be required......» - Luke 12:48

#554 « The ability to learn is the most important quality a leader can have.» - Padmasree Warrior

#555 « Things may come to those who wait, but only the things left by those who hustle.» - Abraham Lincoln

#556 « Twenty-eight years in business and you understand the importance of problem solving and the importance of efficiency, because if you don't become efficient, you don't run a business well, and you are out of business. And I think some of those principles could be applied to leadership in Washington.» - Steve Daines

#557 « Once it gets to a point where it becomes a matter of life and death to occupy a position of leadership or not, with an eye on future opportunities, therein lies the danger.» - Kgalema Motlanthe

#558 « I'll practice as good as I can, but I know that I play even better, with the qualities I have - leadership, my ability to make something happen in games, winning.» - Tim Tebow

#559 « You have to think anyway, so why not think big?» - Donald Trump

#560 « A genuine leader is not a searcher for consensus, but a molder of consensus.» - Martin Luther King Jr.

#561 « We have to go to war against the people who enable the gun violence, the people who stop us from keeping guns out of the hands of mentally unstable people, of felons, and that means the NRA leadership.» - Jerrold Nadler

#562 « Leadership involves finding a parade and getting in front of it.» - John Naisbitt

#563 « Lead, follow, or get out of the way.» - Laurence J. Peter

#564 « Leadership experts and the public alike extol the virtues of transformational leaders - those who set out bold objectives and take risks to change the world. We tend to downplay 'transactional' leaders, whose goals are more modest, as mere managers.» - Joseph Nye

#565 « Leadership can change its mind; leadership can open its eye. Leadership can even be replaced.» - Ehud Barak

#566 « The problem is, is that President Bush and the Republican leadership in the Congress have resisted attempts to increase dramatically our fuel economy standards over the last five years.» - Ed Markey

#567 « Educationists should build the capacities of the spirit of inquiry, creativity, entrepreneurial and moral leadership among students and become their role model.» - A. P. J. Abdul Kalam

#568 « My attitude is never to be satisfied, never enough, never.» - Duke Ellington

#569 « All of the things an arts education gives a young person enhance leadership skills and help raise grades.» - Josh Groban

#570 « I think we need the feminine qualities of leadership, which include attention to aesthetics and the environment, nurturing, affection, intuition and the qualities that make people feel safe and cared for.» - Deepak Chopra

#571 « A leader has the vision and conviction that a dream can be achieved. He inspires the power and energy to get it done.» - Ralph Nader

#572 « Two different styles of leadership. LeBron, very encouraging, bringing everybody along, and Kobe, he's testing you, seeing what you gonna give him. If he gonna get at you, he gonna scream at you, he gonna cuss, he gonna do whatever it is. He had his own way of leading guys as well. It's two different sides. I'm just blessed to see both of them.» - Jordan Clarkson

#573 « Xerox's innovative technology and service offerings - delivered through an expanding distribution system with a lean and flexible business model - continue to solidify our market leadership, driving consistently strong earnings performance.» - Anne M. Mulcahy

#574 « What helps people, helps business.» - Leo Burnett

#575 « Without initiative, leaders are simply workers in leadership positions.» - Bo Bennett

#576 « Limitations live only in our minds. But if we use our imaginations, our possibilities become limitless.» - Jamie Paolinetti

#577 « Challenges make you discover things about yourself that you never really knew.» - Cicely Tyson

#578 « A leader is someone who holds her - or himself accountable for finding the potential in people and processes. » - Brene Brown

#579 « There has not yet been a major ground offensive battle... There are, we know, negotiations going on between the opposition forces and the Taliban leadership for surrender.» - Peter Pace

#580 « Leadership is about encouraging women to break their silence and tell their stories to the world.» - Zainab Salbi

#581 « Leadership is the capacity to translate vision into reality.» - Warren G. Bennis

#582 « Beginning under the Roman Empire, intellectual leadership in the West had been provided by Christianity. In the middle ages, who invented the first universities - in Paris, Oxford, Cambridge? The church.» - Nancy Pearcey

#583 « Without initiative, leaders are simply workers in leadership positions.» - Bo Bennett

#584 « The amount of good luck coming your way depends on your willingness to act.» - Barbara Sher

#585 « So long as the global economy continues to recover, that remains Obama's No. 1 claim to successful leadership. Nothing else even comes close.» - Thomas P.M. Barnett

#586 « Labor, under their current leadership, want to be the Downtown Abbey party when it comes to educational opportunity. They think working class children should stick to the station in life they were born into - they should be happy to be recognized for being good with their hands and not presume to get above themselves.» - Michael Gove

#587 « Business leaders cannot be bystanders.» - Howard Schultz

#588 « It's a different era. Our job now is to show leadership and vision and to help the next generation of artists.» - Karen Kain

#589 « I have a different vision of leadership. A leadership is someone who brings people together.» - George W. Bush

#590 « Where there is no vision, there is no hope.» - George Washington Carver

#591 « Depend upon it, sir, when a man knows he is to be hanged in a fortnight, it concentrates his mind wonderfully.» - Samuel Johnson

#592 « Obstacles are things a person sees when he takes his eyes off his goal.» - E. Joseph Cossman

#593 « Do not withhold good from those to whom it is due, when it is in the power of your hand to do so.» - Proverbs 3:27

#594 « In addition to removing our democratically elected government, Israel wants to sow dissent among Palestinians by claiming that there is a serious leadership rivalry among us. I am compelled to dispel this notion definitively.» - Ismail Haniyeh

#595 « Leadership is by far the most important quality when it comes to making a show that's going to last and of superb quality, something classy and fun.» - Andre Braugher

#596 « Boone Pickens should be commended for his leadership on American energy security, and for bringing Ted Turner along on some sensible approaches to enhancing it.» - Frank Gaffney

#597 « When you're in a leadership role, you can never please all of the people all of the time. There's also a lot of responsibility that goes along with it that others may not realize.» - Joyce Meyer

#598 « Lead, follow, or get out of the way.» - Laurence J. Peter

#599 « Wise leaders generally have wise counselors because it takes a wise person themselves to distinguish them.» - Diogenes of Sinope

#600 « Many corporate leaders and employees have the right intentions, but it can be overwhelming when you consider how everything is affected from leadership styles, to organizational structure, to employee engagement, to customer service an marketplace.» - Simon Mainwaring

#601 « To handle yourself, use your head; to handle others, use your heart.» - Eleanor Roosevelt

#602 « I'm so grateful to have been able to go to the world and tell the story of South African women and South African children. As I stood there for Miss Universe, I spoke about leadership and I spoke about empowering young women and young boys as well.» - Zozibini Tunzi

#603 « Leadership is the art of getting someone else to do something you want to be done because he wants to do it.» - Dwight D. Eisenhower

#604 « There is a sense of call to take leadership roles. You're serving people and submitting to God as best you can.» - Richard Foster

#605 « If everyone is thinking alike, then somebody isn't thinking.» - George S. Patton

#606 « Constant, gentle pressure is my preferred technique for leadership, guidance, and coaching.» - Danny Meyer

#607 « Uncertainty is a permanent part of the leadership landscape. It never goes away.» - Andy Stanley

#608 « Some people feel, you make your case, if they listen to you, fine, if they don't, that's it. That's not what leadership is. Leadership is trying to continue to make a case.» - Anthony Fauci

#609 « The last of human freedoms» - the ability to choose one’s attitude in a given set of circumstances.

#610 « I think America has a responsibility to maintain its leadership in technology and its moral leadership in the world, to explore, to seek knowledge.» - Gene Cernan

#611 « The secret is to work less as individuals and more as a team. As a coach, I play not my eleven best, but my best eleven.» - Knute Rockne

#612 « Most Christian leadership is exercised by people who do not know how to develop healthy, intimate relationships and have opted for power and control instead. Many Christian empire-builders have been people unable to give and receive love.» - Henri Nouwen

#613 « The cautious seldom err.» - Confucius

#614 « If a guy is intimidated by a woman in leadership, he has real problems with his own concepts of masculinity. That's a harsh statement, but I believe it to be true.» - Tony Campolo

#615 « Hold yourself responsible for a higher standard than anybody expects of you. Never excuse yourself.» - Henry Ward Beecher

#616 « No wind serves him who addresses his voyage to no certain port.» - Michel de Montaigne

#617 « Great things are done by a series of small things brought together.» - Van Gogh

#618 « The young people I teach now know they are being sold down the river before we even start studying the trends and numbers. That's the toughest part of being a high school economics teacher... being a witness when our children realize that the greatest deficit of all is a deficit of leadership.» - Kurt Bills

#619 « There is only one thing that makes a dream impossible to achieve: the fear of failure.» - Paulo Coelho, The Alchemist

#620 « Be careful the environment you choose for it will shape you; be careful the friends you choose for you will become like them.» - W. Clement Stone

#621 « If your actions inspire others to dream more, learn more, do more and become more, you are a leader.» - John Quincy Adams

#622 « If you command wisely, you'll be obeyed cheerfully.» - Thomas Fuller

#623 « Every time I would give a talk, someone would say, 'You ought to go into politics.' I prefer to call it government leadership. My life has taken me to places where I have experiences that I think I can share. A lot of times, we see people who are career politicians. I'm not the conventional candidate, nor do I want to be.» - Brad Wenstrup

#624 « A leader is one who, out of madness or goodness, volunteers to take upon himself the woe of the people. There are few men so foolish, hence the erratic quality of leadership in the world.» - John Updike

#625 « So here's the question: Without a change in leadership, why would the next four years be any different from the last four years?» - Paul Ryan

#626 « We need real leadership, Democrat, Republican and independent to stand up and say, we have to live within our means.» - Tom Coburn

#627 « When the Islamic revolution began in 1979 under the leadership of Ayatollah Khomeini, it aroused considerable admiration in the Arab street. It presented a model of organised popular action that deposed one of the region's most tyrannical regimes. The people of the region discerned in this revolution new hope for freedom and change.» - Wadah Khanfar

#628 « Woe to the shepherds who are destroying and scattering the sheep of my pasture! declares the Lord.» - Jeremiah 23:1

#629 « If your actions inspire others to dream more, learn more, do more and become more, you are a leader.» - John Quincy Adams

#630 « Enthusiasm is the most important thing in life.» - Tennessee Williams

#631 « We are watching industries crumble, Wall Street firms disappear, unemployment spike, and unprecedented government intervention. And our designated opinion leaders want to know: Is Obama up this week? Is he down? And is his leadership style more like Bill Clinton's, or Abraham Lincoln's?» - Thomas Frank

#632 « I am deeply honored by the opportunity to lead Intel. We have amazing assets, tremendous talent, and an unmatched legacy of innovation and execution. I look forward to working with our leadership team and employees worldwide to continue our proud legacy while moving even faster into ultra-mobility to lead Intel into the next era.» - Brian Krzanich

#633 « Doing what is right isn't the problem. It is knowing what is right.» - Lyndon B. Johnson

#634 « We never used to blink at taking a leadership role in the world. And we understood leadership often required something other than drones and bombs. We accepted global leadership not just for humanitarian reasons, but also because it was in our own best interest. We knew we couldn't isolate ourselves from trouble. There was no place to hide.» - Robert Reich

#635 « I suppose leadership at one time meant muscles, but today it means getting along with people.» - Mohandas Gandhi

#636 « I believe it is time for new leadership that is able to leave the '70s behind.» - Kim Campbell

#637 « Good leadership consists of showing average people how to do the work of superior people.» - John D. Rockefeller

#638 « I know of no single formula for success. But over the years I have observed that some attributes of leadership are universal and are often about finding ways of encouraging people to combine their efforts, their talents, their insights, their enthusiasm and their inspiration to work together.» - Queen Elizabeth II

#639 « I'm floored that the House leadership would turn its back on job creation for Mississippians.» - Haley Barbour

#640 « The bottom line is, I hear my donors, I hear our base out there, I hear the leadership. And we're taking steps to make sure that we're even more - how shall we say it - fiscally conservative in our spending and certainly making sure the dollars are there when it's time to run our campaigns.» - Michael Steele

#641 « Leadership is about doing what you know is right - even when a growing din of voices around you is trying to convince you to accept what you know to be wrong.» - Bob Ehrlich

#642 « I want to organize so that women see ourselves as people who are entitled to power, entitled to leadership.» - Patricia Ireland

#643 « You cannot be a leader, and ask other people to follow you, unless you know how to follow, too.» - Sam Rayburn

#644 « My life path number is 7. One of the qualities is leadership. If I'm not being a leader, I'm not doing what I'm supposed to be doing.» - NLE Choppa

#645 « Uncertainty is a permanent part of the leadership landscape. It never goes away.» - Andy Stanley

#646 « For any movement to gain momentum, it must start with a small action. This action becomes multiplied by the masses, and is made tangible when leadership changes course due to the weight of the movement's voice.» - Adam Braun

#647 « The nicest thing about standards is that there are so many of them to choose from.» - Ken Olsen

#648 « If you command wisely, you'll be obeyed cheerfully.» - Thomas Fuller

#649 « Time is neutral and does not change things. With courage and initiative, leaders change things.» - Rev. Jesse Jackson

#650 « China is the largest and most ancient of Asiatic countries, but it is not for us boastfully to talk of her right to a position of 'leadership' among those countries.» - Chiang Kai-shek

#651 « Leadership is practiced not so much in words as in attitude and in actions.» - Harold S. Geneen

#652 « As members of Congress, we take an oath to uphold the Constitution and bear true faith and allegiance to the United States, not the Republican or Democratic party. I have been willing to stand up to my own leadership when it's in the national interest.» - Jackie Speier

#653 « I don't run a non-profit. There are lots of non-profits in America - in Detroit, parts of Wall Street, etc. I run a not for profit. We're a business. The only difference is that instead of selling soap or sneakers, we sell hope and leadership.» - Nancy Lublin

#654 « I believe that the capacity that any organisation needs is for leadership to appear anywhere it is needed, when it is needed.» - Margaret J. Wheatley

#655 « I think a captain is someone who captains on the cricket field but, most of the leadership that happens is off the cricket field. It's very easy to captain people on the cricket field, but if you can start leading them off the cricket field, and show them that trust, what you have in them.» - Gautam Gambhir

#656 « I think it is important to ask ourselves as citizens, not as Democrats attacking the administration, but as citizens, whether a world power can really provide global leadership on the basis of fear and anxiety?» - Zbigniew Brzezinski

#657 « I emphasize self-esteem, self-confidence, and dignity, not as an ideal, but as a real test of community organization. Without leadership development, community organizations do not have staying power.» - Paul Wellstone

#658 « The leadership lost its nerve. Instead of taking the lead in the reform movement... they pulled the plug on it. They tried and are still trying to return the church to the dry ice of the previous century and a half.» - Andrew Greeley

#659 « It's only under Prime Minister Narendra Modi's leadership that the country can foresee a bright future.» - Nirmala Sitharaman

#660 « I am proud of the President's leadership. I am proud to support him in saying: Yes, we are going to do what is necessary now when it is less painful and less expensive.» - Kay Bailey Hutchison

#661 « The more that social democracy develops, grows, and becomes stronger, the more the enlightened masses of workers will take their own destinies, the leadership of their movement, and the determination of its direction into their own hands.» - Rosa Luxemburg

#662 « There is an irresistible demand to strengthen the leadership of the constructive forces of the world at the present momentous time. This is true because of stupendous, almost unbelievable changes which have taken place in recent years on every continent.» - John Mott

#663 « We know that al Qaeda in the Arabian Peninsula has some very dangerous, very important leaders who are tied directly to the top leadership of al Qaeda central, including a man who was formerly Osama bin Laden's secretary.» - Richard Engel

#664 « They always say time changes things, but you actually have to change them yourself.» - Andy Warhol

#665 « Dr. King's leadership reaffirmed the promise of our democracy: that everyday people, working together, have the power to change our government and our institutions for the better.» - Maria Cantwell

#666 « For where your treasure is, there will your heart be also.» - Matthew 6:21

#667 « This administration and the leadership in Congress appear to be intent on valuing wealth over work, thereby placing working families at a distinct disadvantage.» - Tim Bishop

#668 « Roosevelt was the one who had the vision to change our policy from isolationism to world leadership. That was a terrific revolution. Our country's never been the same since.» - W. Averell Harriman

#669 « On the other hand, the waging of peace as a science, as an art, is in its infancy. But we can trace its growth, its steady progress, and the time will come when there will be particular individuals designated to assume responsibility for and leadership of this movement.» - Fredrik Bajer

#670 « I suppose leadership at one time meant muscles; but today it means getting along with people.» - Mohandas K. Gandhi

#671 « We need the kind of leadership exemplified by President Kennedy to just do it! But we must do it as good stewards, aggressively exerting control over the moon. We can best do this by going there.» - Wilson Greatbatch

#672 « As the Palestinian leadership never seems to pay any penalty for its words, America's seriousness about the peace process is in doubt.» - Elliott Abrams

#673 « We're in a leadership position in sports. People look up to the National Football League.» - Roger Goodell

#674 « In the end, North Korea's conduct may change only when its leadership does.» - Antony Blinken

#675 « Whoever loves instruction loves knowledge, But he who hates correction is stupid.» - Proverbs 12:1

#676 « Charlatanism of some degree is indispensable to effective leadership.» - Eric Hoffer

#677 « Leadership should be born out of the understanding of the needs of those who would be affected by it.» - Marian Anderson

#678 « In terms of leadership, you've got to allow for people to be amazing and to contribute in a way that's meaningful. You can't hold on so tight that people don't get a chance to do what they do best.» - Nahnatchka Khan

#679 « I think we need leadership that helps us remember that part of what we are about is caring about more than the person right next to us, but the folks across the way.» - Anna Deavere Smith

#680 « The price of leadership is strange.» - Tom Izzo

#681 « Message to all you crazed parents desperately hiring tutors and padding your kid's thin resume: Chillax. Attending an elite college is no guarantee of leadership, life success, or earnings potential.» - Nina Easton

#682 « The problem is not Hamas, the problem is not people. The root of the problem is Islam itself as an idea, as an idea. And about Hamas as an organization, of course, the Hamas leadership, including my father, they're responsible; they're responsible for all the violence that happened from the organization.» - Mosab Hassan Yousef

#683 « The democratic idealist is prone to make light of the whole question of standards and leadership because of his unbounded faith in the plain people.» - Irving Babbitt

#684 « One of the tests of leadership is the ability to recognize a problem before it becomes an emergency.» - Arnold Glasow

#685 « Having served in the Nixon Administration, I am well aware of how the political leadership of an administration can try to politicize the civil service, including law enforcement.» - Frank Wolf

#686 « I have spent years as a leadership coach to the very wealthy and have been able to get behind the eyes of some of the world's best, studying the minute details of what makes a person great.» - Robin S. Sharma

#687 « You may be disappointed if you fail, but you are doomed if you don't try.» - Beverly Sills

#688 « Churches need to figure out how they will address the spiritual lives of their staffs and leadership teams.» - John Ortberg

#689 « Problems are only opportunities in work clothes.» - Henry J. Kaiser

#690 « Leadership is based on a spiritual quality; the power to inspire, the power to inspire others to follow.» - Vince Lombardi

#691 « There's plenty of room at the top, but there's no room to sit down» - Helen Downey

#692 « Democrats have no agenda, no plan for the future, and no sense of leadership.» - Jeff Miller

#693 « Outside of my family, I was always inspired by true heroic stories of leadership and survival. For example, the story of the Shackleton expedition, when their ship became lodged in the Antarctic ice pack while exploring.» - Christina Koch

#694 « The action of Rosa Parks, the words and leadership of Dr. King inspired me. I was deeply inspired. I wanted to do something.» - John Lewis

#695 « World War II had been such a tremendous success story for this country that the political and military leadership began to assume that they would prevail simply because of who they were. We were like the British at the turn of the 19th century.» - Neil Sheehan

#696 « Affirmation without discipline is the beginning of delusion.» - R. Buckminster Fuller

#697 « The House Republican leadership has simply run out of ideas.» - Jan Schakowsky

#698 « I vote my conscience first and my constituents next, regardless of the direction of our leadership.» - Tom Graves

#699 « I was brought up in a family of leaders, and I think leadership is a life sentence. I like changing things that will shape the future.» - Jenny Shipley

#700 « A good plan violently executed now is better than a perfect plan executed next week.» - George Patton

#701 « If I fail to remove Marcos and vindicate the people's verdict by peaceful, nonviolent action, my methods will be discredited. And if anger persists, I will be marginalized, and others will take over leadership of the movement.» - Corazon Aquino

#702 « One must be convinced to convince, to have enthusiasm to stimulate the others.» - Stefan Zweig

#703 « There are certain skills that business people have that are - that are, in fact, helpful in - when it comes to being in political leadership.» - Rick Santorum

#704 « Life is the art of drawing sufficient conclusions from insufficient premises.» - Samuel Butler

#705 « High expectations are the key to everything.» - Sam Walton

#706 « The leadership instinct you are born with is the backbone. You develop the funny bone and the wishbone that go with it.» - Elaine Agather

#707 « When I was growing up, we were taught in school that North Koreans, and especially the North Korean leadership, were all devils.» - Park Chan-wook

#708 « We need safe communities that are free from methamphetamine and a federal commitment to stand next to state leadership and law enforcement in the fight against this epidemic.» - Rick Larsen

#709 « When placed in command, take charge.» - Norman Schwarzkopf

#710 « The task of leadership is not to put greatness into humanity, but to elicit it, for the greatness is already there.» - John Buchan

#711 « Never give an order that can't be obeyed.» - Douglas MacArthur

#712 « I am convinced that your Mayor must take the leadership role in education too.» - Alan Autry

#713 « Our democracy poses problems and these problems must and shall be solved by courageous leadership.» - Charles Edison

#714 « From his lifetime of experience as a turnaround expert in private equity to his experience with the turnaround mission of the Olympics to his successful term as a blue state GOP governor, Romney can point to a record of bipartisan leadership and achievement that Obama can only talk about.» - Margaret Hoover

#715 « I cannot give you the formula for success, but I can give you the formula for failure, which is: Try to please everybody.» - Herbert Swope

#716 « Choose always the way that seems the best, however rough it may be; custom will soon render it easy and agreeable.» - Pythagoras

#717 « The only person you are destined to become is the person you decide to be.» - Ralph Waldo Emerson

#718 « We do not need international help to stop corruption, we need strong Louisiana Leadership.» - David Vitter

#719 « I forgot to shake hands and be friendly. It was an important lesson about leadership.» - Lee Iacocca

#720 « A good leader must hate the wrong thing more than they hate the pain of doing the right thing.» - Angela Jiang

#721 « I mean, Emily Harris was his wife. And she seemed to resent his leadership, but on the other hand, she felt like a good soldier, that he had to be the leader.» - Patty Hearst

#722 « Leadership is an intense journey into yourself. You can use your own style to get anything done. It's about being self-aware. Every morning, I look in the mirror and say, 'I could have done three things better yesterday.'« - Jeffrey R. Immelt

#723 « This obsession with leadership... It's not neutral; it's American, this idea of the heroic leader who comes in on a white horse to save the day. I think it's killing American companies.» - Henry Mintzberg

#724 « Bipartisanship isn't an option anymore; it is a requirement. The American people have divided responsibility for leadership right down the middle.» - Tom Daschle

#725 « The quality of a leader is reflected in the standards they set for themselves.» - Ray Kroc

#726 « I definitely wasn't cool in high school. I really wasn't. I did belong to many of the clubs and was in leadership on yearbook and did the musical theater route, so I had friends in all areas. But I certainly did not know what to wear, did not know how to do my hair, all those things.» - Dianna Agron

#727 « I think leadership is knowing what you want to achieve and then purposefully and sensibly taking steps to achieve it, remembering always that you have got to bring people with you if you are seeking to be a successful political leader.» - Tony Abbott

#728 « Too many of us are not living our dreams because we are living our fears.» - Les Brown

#729 « Leadership is intangible, and therefore no weapon ever designed can replace it.» - Omar N. Bradley

#730 « Above all else, guard your heart, for everything you do flows from it.» - Proverbs 4:23

#731 « I'm a pragmatist. I think, as a woman, you have to be more careful. You have to be more communal, you have to say yes to more things than men, you have to worry about things that men don't have to worry about. But once we get enough women into leadership, we can break stereotypes down. If you lead, you get to decide.» - Sheryl Sandberg

#732 « When the world is in the midst of change, when adversity and opportunity are almost indistinguishable, this is the time for visionary leadership and when leaders need to look beyond the survival needs of those they're serving.» - Chip Conley

#733 « America must not abdicate its global leadership role in the climate crisis to countries like China.» - Mazie Hirono

#734 « You can't be brave if you've only had wonderful things happen to you.» - Mary Tyler Moore

#735 « When President Obama was in the Senate, when he was a U.S. senator, he voted against raising the debt ceiling. And he said it was a lack of leadership that had brought us to this point.» - Cathy McMorris Rodgers

#736 « To improve humanity's chances of survival, it is critical that Canada assume a leadership role, first ramping up our own ambition and then pushing for more ambition overall in global negotiations.» - Elizabeth May

#737 « Well, I think that - I think leadership's always been about two main things: imagination and courage.» - Paul Keating

#738 « If you faint in the day of adversity, Your strength is small.» - Proverbs 24:10

#739 « I'm not up on the Internet, but I hear that is a democratic possibility. People can connect with each other. I think people are ready for something, but there is no leadership to offer it to them. People are ready to say, 'Yes, we are part of a world.'« - Studs Terkel

#740 « The world need strong leadership for women's rights.» - Isabella Lovin

#741 « Research has shown that the perceived style of leadership is by far the most important thing to most voters in evaluating officeholders and candidates.» - Robert Teeter

#742 « I believe in servant leadership, and the servant always asks, 'Where am I needed most?'« - Mike Pence

#743 « I recognize we will pay more attention when we have different leadership.» - Octavia E. Butler

#744 « The most effective way to lead is to lead from within.» - Lolly Daskal

#745 « Through leadership of the fight against French colonialism, Ho Chi Minh had made a name for himself in the international political arena.» - Nguyen Cao Ky

#746 « And the whole world, the whole world that believes in freedom, whether you're talking about personal freedom, economic freedom, religious freedom, they look to the United States for leadership; and you're part of that leadership.» - Don Nickles

#747 « I have never been afraid to stand up to the leadership on issues where we disagree. If you chose to keep Cambridge Labour, then I can continue to press the Government for the things that matter to you, in a way that members of the opposition are unable to.» - Anne Campbell

#748 « Every time you have to speak, you are auditioning for leadership.» - James Humes

#749 « Every act of conscious learning requires the willingness to suffer an injury to one's self-esteem. That is why young children, before they are aware of their own self-importance, learn so easily.» - Thomas Szasz

#750 « There was no imminent threat. This was made up in Texas, announced in January to the Republican leadership that war was going to take place and was going to be good politically. This whole thing was a fraud.» - Edward Kennedy

#751 « If the highest aim of a captain were to preserve his ship, he would keep it in port forever.» - Thomas Aquinas

#752 « I alone cannot change the world, but I can cast a stone across the water to create many ripples.» - Mother Teresa

#753 « One of the problems in the biotech world is the lack of women in leadership roles, and I'd like to see that change by walking the walk.» - Jennifer Doudna

#754 « 'Good, better, best. Never let it rest. 'Til your good is better and your better is best.'» - St Jerome

#755 « He who wishes to be obeyed must know how to command.» - Niccolò Machiavelli

#756 « China and India will take the global leadership on climate change: they are suffering for it.» - Malcolm Turnbull

#757 « I think that bold leadership sells.» - Sean Duffy

#758 « We in the press, by our power, can actually undermine leadership.» - Christiane Amanpour

#759 « The Washington leadership has put aside non-proliferation programmes and devoted its energies and resources to driving the country to war by extraordinary deceit, then trying to manage the catastrophe it created in Iraq.» - Noam Chomsky

#760 « Doing is a quantum leap from imagining.» - Barbara Sher

#761 « A man who wants to lead the orchestra must turn his back on the crowd.» - Max Lucado

#762 « Music is all about leadership and there ain't really a lot of leaders.» - Young Jeezy

#763 « Preparing our city to achieve its destiny will require strong leadership.» - Thomas Menino

#764 « Mandela's heroism is the heroism of a man who suffered so badly for what he thought of as freedom. And yet when he had the upper hand he has this incredible self-control and these incredible leadership qualities.» - Bono

#765 « I've made some films for the military that are teaching things like cultural awareness and leadership issues, that sort of stuff. And try to, in essence, look at what training they're doing and say, 'This is how you can improve the training from a humanistic point of view.'« - Carl Weathers

#766 « The very essence of leadership is that you have to have vision. You can't blow an uncertain trumpet.» - Theodore Hesburgh

#767 « A good general not only sees the way to victory; he also knows when victory is impossible.» - Polybius

#768 « It's really necessary for the United States to continue to give strong leadership to the Middle East peace process, supported by European countries at the same time.» - William Hague

#769 « We live in a time where government is not a leadership thing, it's more a business that's out there and running riot, so I guess the people have to go out there and say stuff.» - Yahoo Serious

#770 « Leadership is a choice, not a position.» - Stephen R. Covey

#771 « Strive not to be a success, but rather to be of value.» - Albert Einstein

#772 « Now, if we look at the way in which the labor movement itself has evolved over the last couple of decades, we see increasing numbers of black people who are in the leadership of the labor movement and this is true today.» - Angela Davis

#773 « Leaders don't inflict pain, they share pain.» - Max Depree

#774 « To have long» - term success as a coach or in any position of leadership, you have to be obsessed in some way. Pat Riley

#775 « In the long march of history, at least two poles of attraction and antagonism have been the norm in world politics. Rarely has only one nation carried the burden of leadership. The unipolar world of the 21st century, dominated for the past two decades by the United States, is a historical anomaly.» - Eskinder Nega

#776 « Actions, such as the designation of National Childhood Obesity Awareness Month, spring from First Lady Michelle Obama's leadership of efforts to end childhood obesity within this generation.» - Richard Carmona

#777 « Leadership is a choice you make, not a place you sit.» - Robert F. Tucker

#778 « The Divine Thing that made itself the foundation of the Church does not seem, to judge by his comments on the religious leadership of his day, to have hoped much from officers of a church.» - Charles Williams

#779 « I think as a leader, you just take accountability. That's what leadership is. Leadership is taking accountability yourself and holding others to the same standard, regardless of what's going on.» - Jason Kelce

#780 « Priesthood lessons are regularly devoted to topics of family leadership, and quorum leaders everywhere are feeling more and more their responsibility to teach and train their quorum members to be better husbands and fathers.» - Joseph B. Wirthlin

#781 « People look for their leadership to lead.» - Mick Cornett

#782 « Bill Gates can't control a high-level-energy dog, because his energy is very low, very calm. Very intellectual. A dog doesn't see that as leadership.» - Cesar Millan

#783 « So whatever you wish that others would do to you, do also to them, for this is the Law and the Prophets.» - Matthew 7:12

#784 « Leadership consists of picking good men and helping them do their best.» - Chester W. Nimitz

#785 « Even after such milestones as Kathryn Bigelow winning an Oscar, there still seem to be few women in leadership roles.» - Julia Stiles

#786 « They said it was impossible to touch the third rail of politics, to take on public-sector unions and to reform a pension and health benefits system that was headed to bankruptcy. But with bipartisan leadership, we saved taxpayers» 132 billion dollars over 30 years and saved retirees their pensions. We did it.» - Chris Christie

#787 « Surround yourself with great people; delegate authority; get out of the way.» - Ronald Reagan

#788 « Leadership is an ever - evolving position. » - Mike Krzyzewski

#789 « 'Anyone who has ever made anything of importance was disciplined.'» - Andrew Hendrixson

#790 « Vocational education programs have made a real difference in the lives of countless young people nationwide; they build self-confidence and leadership skills by allowing students to utilize their unique gifts and talents.» - Conrad Burns

#791 « Servant leadership is the foundation and the secret of Sam Walton's ability to achieve team synergy.» - Michael Bergdahl

#792 « A leader is a dealer in hope.» - Napoleon Bonaparte

#793 « Only be you strong, and very courageous, then you will make your way prosperous, and then you will have good success.» - Joshua 1:7

#794 « It takes leadership to improve safety. And I started off the movement in my time, but the person who has done more over the past 20 to 30 years and who has led it is Professor Sid Watkins.» - Jackie Stewart

#795 « People who enjoy meetings should not be in charge of anything.» - Thomas Sowell

#796 « There are no office hours for leaders.» - Cardinal J. Gibbons

#797 « I've always believed that government tends to screw up whatever it touches, but Obama in particular seemed different. He understood tech issues that left the other candidates bewildered. Part of it may be his age. But whatever the reason, I had real hope that he could help lead us into a new century of technology leadership and growth.» - Michael Arrington

#798 « Nixon was an awful president in many ways, including in some of his foreign-policy choices. But he left no doubt that foreign policy and America's leadership in the world outside its borders was of paramount importance to him.» - John Podhoretz

#799 « He's a novice, but he's had these - he's experienced in leadership in tight circumstances. He started - he dropped the first bomb, led the first air strike into North Vietnam.» - James Stockdale

#800 « Leadership in telecommunications is also essential, since we are now in the age of e-commerce.» - Michael Oxley

#801 « I think our leadership is now seized of the fact that we have a problem with the youth vote and it might be an idea to get into an intelligent place, both in policy making and in terms of the presentation of our values around freedom and responsibility.» - Crispin Blunt

#802 « Under the leadership of this President, the state of the union is not strong. We are being pulled apart rather than pulling together. Our democracy is suffering from the choices being made, and yet we are offered the same tired excuses and unrealistic analyses.» - Jose Serrano

#803 « In terms of the principles of politics, I think I understand well. Thailand needs someone who has leadership, who has the management skills to help the country.» - Yingluck Shinawatra

#804 « In an age when stagecraft, gauzy themes, and sound-bites have too often been substituted for leadership, Bill Clinton as a candidate made it essential to campaigning to take the specifics of governance seriously. Practical solutions were 'in;' ideology was 'out.'« - Sylvia Mathews Burwell

#805 « The signs of outstanding leadership appear primarily among the followers. Are the followers reaching their potential? Are they learning? Serving? Do they achieve the required results? Do they change with grace? Manage conflict?» - Max de Pree

#806 « Obama is thoroughly mixed up with all these things he's got. He's got to solve Libya. He's got to solve Afghanistan. He's everywhere. And this nation, I don't know why it's not showing the leadership and capacity to attend different issues at the same time.» - Vicente Fox

#807 « The BJP members and their leadership have realized that the Bahujan Samaj Party's policies are not anti-upper caste.» - Mayawati

#808 « Simply let your 'Yes' be 'Yes,' and your 'No,' 'No'; anything beyond this comes from the evil one.» - Matthew 5:37

#809 « The art of leadership is saying no, not saying yes. It is very easy to say yes.» - Tony Blair

#810 « You're only as good as the people you hire.» - Ray Kroc

#811 « You only have to do a very few things right in your life so long as you don't do too many things wrong.» - Warren Buffett

#812 « We design our own programmes; we take leadership. Of course the donors come in to support us, to complement our efforts. Our responsibility to the donors is about accountability: about how we use that money. If somebody gives you his money, definitely he will be interested in knowing how you spend the money.» - Jakaya Kikwete

#813 « California is a very important state. As goes California, so goes the nation. We need to have strong leadership. Someone who can hit the ground running.» - Xavier Becerra

#814 « It is sad that the Republican leadership is not as interested as they say they are in protecting the institution of marriage as they are in waging a campaign to divide and distract the American people from the real issues that need to be addressed.» - Kendrick Meek

#815 « Mahatma Gandhi was someone who demonstrated the tremendous power of leadership by example.» - N. R. Narayana Murthy

#816 « The task of the leader is to get their people from where they are to where they have not been.» - Henry Kissinger

#817 « I've learned that positive thinking and encouragement are essential for leadership and progress.» - Richard M. DeVos

#818 « Leadership is getting someone to do what they don't want to do, to achieve what they want to achieve.» - Tom Landry

#819 « The Chinese public is deeply nationalist, which matters to China's unelected political leadership as much as U.S. nationalism does to American politicians. As China becomes the world's largest economy, there is meaningful public pressure for its power status to advance in parallel. Any alternative would be humiliating.» - Noah Feldman

#820 « Now Moses was a very humble man, more humble than anyone else on the face of the earth.» - Numbers 12:3

#821 « It is rare to find a business partner who is selfless. If you are lucky it happens once in a lifetime.» - Michael Eisner

#822 « He who has great power should use it lightly.» - Seneca

#823 « I think most Americans understand that we went through a period in which American leadership was judged quite critically internationally.» - Susan Rice

#824 « The growth and development of people is the highest calling of leadership.» - Harvey S. Firestone

#825 « We must recognize that as the dominant power in the world we have a special responsibility. In addition to protecting our national interests, we must take the leadership in protecting the common interests of humanity.» - George Soros

#826 « Great companies in the way they work, start with great leaders.» - Steve Ballmer

#827 « Leadership is the key to 99 percent of all successful efforts.» - Erskine Bowles

#828 « Leadership is about being a servant first.» - Allen West

#829 « Leadership is a privilege to better the lives of others. It is not an opportunity to satisfy personal greed.» - Mwai Kibaki

#830 « I have spent a lifetime watching kids make mistakes because they were not trained or well led or properly motivated to do well. I never faulted the kids; rather, I saw opportunity to train, to motivate, to improve leadership - not to punish the individual.» - Eric Shinseki

#831 « For many years, Myanmar's leadership was largely shut out from the world of international diplomacy.» - Najib Razak

#832 « I think leadership is something you earn, more through actions than words.» - Ander Crenshaw

#833 « The Leadership Training Institute of America trains and equips young men and women to be leaders with high standards of personal morality and integrity.» - Michael C. Burgess

#834 « Our leadership group has a responsibility to pass on what it means to be a Boomer and play for your country and make sure this program is at its peak knowing the type of talent coming through.» - Patty Mills

#835 « A man who isolates himself seeks his own desire; He rages against all wise judgment.» - Proverbs 18:1

#836 « A good part of my leadership skills is crafted from learning from experiences early in my career that were not positive experiences.» - John Lasseter

#837 « As a vibrant force in civil society, women continue to press for their rights, equal participation in decision-making, and the upholding of the principles of the revolution by the highest levels of leadership in Egypt.» - Michelle Bachelet

#838 « My sports were team sports: ice hockey and baseball. The whole team dynamic is similar in business. Leadership is earned - the captain earns that role; it's not because he's the coach's son. These are all things we know, but in today's world, it's not a bad idea to remind ourselves.» - James McNerney

#839 « I didn't fail the test. I just found 100 ways to do it wrong.» - Benjamin Franklin

#840 « Men make history and not the other way around. In periods where there is no leadership, society stands still. Progress occurs when courageous, skillful leaders seize the opportunity to change things for the better.» - Harry S Truman

#841 « There go my people. I must find out where they are going so I can lead them.» - Alexandre Ledru

#842 « Every morning, I look in the mirror and say, 'I could have done three things better yesterday.'« - Jeffrey R. Immelt

#843 « Education is the mother of leadership.» - Wendell Willkie

#844 « Leadership is more than just managing economic reforms. Leadership means giving broad direction, take up challenges which other people cannot do.» - Ajay Piramal

#845 « Good leadership consists of showing average people how to do the work of superior people.» - John D. Rockefeller

#846 « I look forward to working with our leadership team to advance the causes of smaller government, lower taxes, eliminating terrorism, and providing affordable health care, among other issues.» - Howard Coble

#847 « If you really want the key to success, start by doing the opposite of what everyone else is doing.» - Brad Szollose

#848 « At an unprecedented time with the worst attack ever on our soil, our President displayed extraordinary determination, leadership and resolve when history was thrust upon him and the United States.» - Olympia Snowe

#849 « Leadership can't be fabricated. If it is fabricated and rehearsed, you can't fool the guys in the locker room. So when you talk about leadership, it comes with performance. Leadership comes with consistency.» - Junior Seau

#850 « Get the best people and train them well.» - Scott McNealy

#851 « I know that millions of Americans from all walks of life agree with me that leadership does not mean putting the ear to the ground to follow public opinion, but to have the vision of what is necessary and the courage to make it possible.» - Shirley Chisholm

#852 « Strategic leaders must not get consumed by the operational and tactical side of their work.» - Stephanie S. Mead

#853 « It's not as if our party has a leadership campaign underway.» - Peter MacKay

#854 « As I've progressed in my career, I've come to appreciate - and really value - the other attributes that define a company's success beyond the P&L: great leadership, long-term financial strength, ethical business practices, evolving business strategies, sound governance, powerful brands, values-based decision-making.» - Ursula Burns

#855 « We expect our leaders to be godlike. But I feel that when people try to sanctify leadership, it puts it out of the realm of regular people. And that's where the greatest leaders come from - from the people.» - Katori Hall

#856 « Leadership is solving problems. The day soldiers stop bringing you their problems is the day you have stopped leading them. They have either lost confidence that you can help or concluded you do not care. Either case is a failure of leadership.» - Colin Powell

#857 « The key to being a good manager is keeping the people who hate me away from those who are still undecided.» - Casey Stengel

#858 « Women especially are often asked to choose between being a mother and being a leader. Without adequate policy support, too many women face not only financial barriers to balancing motherhood and leadership, but cultural stigmas too.» - Michelle Wu

#859 « Where there is no vision, there is no hope.» - George Washington Carver

#860 « Leadership is a matter of having people look at you and gain confidence, seeing how you react. If you're in control, they're in control.» - Tom Landry

#861 « Dreaming, after all, is a form of planning.» - Gloria Steinem

#862 « Teaching is a profession in which capacity building should occur at every stage of the career - novices working with accomplished colleagues, skillful teachers sharing their craft, and opportunities for teacher leadership.» - Randi Weingarten

#863 « The job of nation building, the job of nation leadership in a difficult, complex coalition has worked.» - Azim Premji

#864 « I praise loudly, I blame softly.» - Catherine the Great

#865 « Leadership» - leadership is about taking responsibility, not making excuses.

#866 « One of the main ways that leadership stays in power is by, in various ways, convincing people that they should just let those who are in government govern: 'Trust us. Trust me. Just let us take care of things. Stay out of it.' Your opinions don't really matter. You are isolated. You are insignificant.» - Viggo Mortensen

#867 « In government, our chief executives have been lawyers. The great majority of our cabinets and congresses are and have been men trained in the law. They have provided the leadership and the statecraft and the store of strength when it was needed.» - Robert Kennedy

#868 « At the very outset I want to say how the people of America appreciate the steadfast support of the people of Morocco, the leadership of Morocco in our war against terrorism.» - Donald Evans

#869 « A good cult delivers on its promises. A good cult nourishes the needs of its members, has transparency and integrity, and creates provisions for challenging its leadership openly. A good cult expands the freedoms and well-being of its members rather than limits them.» - Philip Zimbardo

#870 « We're here for a reason. I believe a bit of the reason is to throw little torches out to lead people through the dark.» - Whoopi Goldberg

#871 « I believe that it is irresponsible, it is basically part of the crisis of leadership in D.C. to not look at

Social Security and understand that there has got to be a solution posed. We've got to take a look at it and make sure that we create a solution so our seniors aren't left out in the cold.» - Joe Miller

#872 « Every great leader can take you back to a defining moment when they decided to lead.» - John Paul Warren

#873 « So I think that our foreign policy, the president's strong and principled leadership when it comes to the war against terror and foreign policy is going to be an asset.» - Ed Gillespie

#874 « My father's values and vision of this country obviously form everything I have as values and ideals. But this is not the ghost of my father running for the leadership of the Liberal party. This is me.» - Justin Trudeau

#875 « Under President Trump's leadership, illegal immigration was the lowest it had been in 17 years. The Trump administration achieved this success because they understood the actual problems and addressed them.» - Lauren Boebert

#876 « This - the leadership of the mayor is crucial, because it is to the mayor that people will look to provide the vision, the energy, and the sense of confidence in the rebuilding and the recovery.» - Marc Morial

#877 « Mexico has lost its leadership, and a lot of that has to do with its poor performance and the lack of better results in our country.» - Enrique Pena Nieto

#878 « There would not be enough talent that's educated, developed and ready to take on the next leadership challenge, and it would cap our growth. Now we've put programs in place not to have that happen, but that could be a weakness.» - Kevin Rollins

#879 « Leadership contains certain elements of good management, but it requires that you inspire, that you build durable trust. For an organization to be not just good but to win, leadership means evoking participation larger than the job description, commitment deeper than any job contract's wording.» - Stanley A. McChrystal

#880 « Lead yourself whenever your boss' leadership deteriorates. When your boss doesn't praise what you do, praise yourself. When your boss doesn't make you big, make yourself big. Remember, if you have done your best, failure does not count.» - Mario Teguh

#881 « If you act enthusiastic, you will be enthusiastic!» - Dale Carnegie

#882 « Leadership distilled down to 3 words: Make a difference.» - Robin Sharma

#883 « I don't agree with all-male leaderships. Men cannot be left to run things on their own. I think it's a thoroughly bad thing to have a men-only leadership.» - Harriet Harman

#884 « To my mind the election was stolen by George Bush and we have been suffering ever since under this man's leadership.» - Jessica Lange

#885 « I very much believe in values-based leadership and that the values that I believe in and try to govern by are transcendent values.» - Deval Patrick

#886 « Do not follow where the path may lead. Go instead where there is no path and leave a trail.» - Ralph Waldo Emerson

#887 « The moral was, in time of anarchy, tough leadership is the only solution - even though the collateral damage may be heartbreaking. Mrs. Thatcher's strident, take-no prisoners approach was in some ways repugnant, but it was surely necessary.» - Nigel Hamilton

#888 « You have to think anyway, so why not think big?» - Donald Trump

#889 « Sinn Fein has demonstrated the ability to play a leadership role as part of a popular movement towards peace, equality and justice.» - Gerry Adams

#890 « To be persuasive we must be believable; to be believable we must be credible; credible we must be truthful.» - Edward R. Murrow

#891 « I don't care tuppence whether I'm forced into a leadership position or not. I'd much sooner not.» - E. P. Thompson

#892 « As someone who has more than a passing acquaintance with most of the 20th century presidents, I have often thought that their accomplishments have little staying power in shaping popular views of their leadership.» - Robert Dallek

#893 « Leadership is something you earn, something you're chosen for. You can't come in yelling, 'I'm your leader!' If it happens, it's because the other guys respect you.» - Ben Roethlisberger

#894 « Each group and each youngster is different. As a leader or coach, you get to know what they need.» - Mike Krzyzewski

#895 « No act of kindness, however small, is ever wasted.» - Aesop

#896 « The test of leadership is not to put greatness into humanity, but to elicit it, for the greatness is already there.» - James Buchanan

#897 « Grades don't measure tenacity, courage, leadership, guts or whatever you want to call it. Teachers or any other persons in a position of authority should never tell anybody they will not succeed because they did not get all A's in school.» - Thomas J. Stanley

#898 « Whoever guards his mouth and tongue, Keeps his soul from troubles.» - Proverbs 21:23

#899 « I also know that there have been many times in our history when the proximity of an election has induced exactly the kind of leadership and consensus-building that produce progress in our democracy.» - Joe Lieberman

#900 « In terms of having views and being prepared to express them, yes, I think New Zealand's had a leadership role in a lot of things.» - Helen Clark

#901 « But 85 percent of the mosques have extremist leadership in this country. Most Muslims, the overwhelming majority of Muslims, are loyal Americans.» - Peter T. King

#902 « I watched my parents in their leadership callings in the Church and the community. We just grew up knowing that we should serve and do whatever we could do to make things grow.» - Margaret D. Nadauld

#903 « Despite the characterization of some that teaching is an easy job, with short hours and summers off, the fact is that successful, dedicated teachers in the U.S. work long hours for little pay and, in many cases, insufficient support from their leadership.» - Andreas Schleicher

#904 « I was re-elected as general secretary with almost 100 per cent of the vote. And I am very surprised by that. Because I am quite old. I am the oldest member in the leadership of Vietnam. I myself asked to be retired but due to responsibility tasked on me by the party I had to accept.» - Nguyen Phu Trong

#905 « Remember that not getting what you want is sometimes a wonderful stroke of luck.» - Dalai Lama

#906 « Let us not become weary in doing good, for at the proper time we will reap a harvest if we do not give up.» - Galatians 6:9

#907 « 'We Need Leaders Who Are Global Citizens': Former UN Head Ban Ki» - moon on Building an Inclusive World

#908 « It's kind of like those little electric bumper cars where you drive around and see if you can hit the other guy. That's exactly what the country is like now. You no longer have the sense of community. Of loyalty. It's lost its sense of group. It has nothing to do with leadership.» - Paul Newman

#909 « Innovation distinguishes between a leader and a follower.» - Steve Jobs

#910 « The role of leadership is to transform the complex situation into small pieces and prioritize them.» - Carlos Ghosn

#911 « Inclusion and transparency have been mainstays of my leadership. It's about education and reaching out.» - Gabrielle Carteris

#912 « Leadership cannot really be taught. It can only be learned.» - Harold Geneen

#913 « In matters of style, swim with the current; in matters of principle, stand like a rock.» - Thomas Jefferson

#914 « And we urge you, brothers, admonish the idle, encourage the fainthearted, help the weak, be patient with them all.» - 1 Thessalonians 5:14

#915 « It is the responsibility of leadership to provide opportunity, and the responsibility of individuals to contribute.» - William Pollard

#916 « Behold, how good and how pleasant it is for brethren to dwell together in unity!» - Psalms 133:1

#917 « A boss has the title, a leader has the people.» - Simon Sinek

#918 « Flaming enthusiasm, backed up by horse sense and persistence, is the quality that most frequently makes for success.» - Dale Canegie

#919 « Whose leadership, whose judgment, whose values do you want in the White House when that crisis lands like a thud on the Oval Office desk?» - Rahm Emanuel

#920 « Leadership is being the best example you can be for your teammates. The guy that everybody can depend on on a nightly basis.» - DeMarcus Cousins

#921 « The art of leadership is saying no, not yes. It is very easy to say yes.» - Tony Blair

#922 « To add value to others, one must first value others.» - John Maxwell

#923 « Only the guy who isn't rowing has time to rock the boat.» - Jean

#924 « People of India deserve to be complimented for making the 2014 elections a referendum on the misrule of the Congress-led UPA and demonstrating their faith in a proven new leadership.» - Piyush Goyal

#925 « The message of the free world to any potential Palestinian leadership should be a simple one: Embrace democratic reform and we will embrace you.» - Natan Sharansky

#926 « A real leader faces the music even when he doesn't like the tune.» - Arnold H. Glasgow

#927 « When people talk, listen completely.» - Ernest Hemingway

#928 « People more than ever since I can remember are concerned about being out of step and out of line with their political party and won't cross over. There is nobody, man or woman, who wants to be left out, and people are fearful of that. People are fearful of their leadership as well.» - Gary Ackerman

#929 « In one of my recent books, 'The Success Principles,' I taught 64 lessons that help people achieve what they want out of life. From taking nothing less than 100 percent responsibility for your life to empowering others, these are the fundamentals to success - and to great leadership.» - Jack Canfield

#930 « The great leaders have always stage-managed their effects.» - Charles de Gaulle

#931 « Leadership involves finding a parade and getting in front of it.» - John Naisbitt

#932 « All the leadership positions that I have had have one common denominator: none has required that I give up my science work.» - Mildred Dresselhaus

#933 « A big part of leadership is just being comfortable with the fact that some decisions really are only yours.» - Helene D. Gayle

#934 « Leadership is the capacity to translate vision into reality.» - Warren Bennis

#935 « The sentiments in Hawaii about Washington's failure of leadership are no different than the rest of the country.» - Ed Case

#936 « The best way to have a good idea is to have a lot of ideas.» - Linus Pauling

#937 « To have long term success as a coach or in any position of leadership, you have to be obsessed in some way.» - Pat Riley

#938 « Management is the art of making problems so interesting that everyone wants to get to work and deal with them.» - Paul Hawken

#939 « Over the years, I have studied church history as well as the contemporary church, and I noticed how rare it is for a God-glorifying transition of leadership to take place in a local church.» - C. J. Mahaney

#940 « When you look at a Congress that has an 84 percent disapproval rating, that means that for the most part, the people of this country, and certainly California, are looking for new leadership.» - Elizabeth Emken

#941 « You have to lead people gently toward what they already know is right.» - Phil Crosby

#942 « I think too much of my leadership is done the bad way.» - Paul Pierce

#943 « Success isn't about how much money you make; it's about the difference you make in people's lives.» - Michelle Obama

#944 « House Republican leadership have refused to allow a clean minimum wage vote. Close to 15 million Americans will be affected if we did this. Do Republicans really expect a family to live on less than» 11,000 a year?» - Bill Pascrell

#945 « Under the leadership of President Bush and Vice President Cheney, the United States has given up the moral high ground that we used to occupy as an international leader.» - Marty Meehan

#946 « Where there is no guidance the people fall, But in abundance of counselors there is victory.» - Proverbs 11:14

#947 « A person who never made a mistake never tried anything new.» - Albert Einstein

#948 « By providing outstanding economic leadership, this country can wage its attack successfully - and can thereby build the foundations of a peaceful world.» - James Forrestal

#949 « A man always has two reasons for doing anything: a good reason and the real reason.» - J. P. Morgan

#950 « A leader who doesn't hesitate before he sends his nation into battle is not fit to be a leader.» - Golda Meir

#951 « Obstacles are things a person sees when he takes his eyes off his goal.» - E. Joseph Cossman

#952 « Great leaders create more leaders, not followers.» - Roy T. Bennett

#953 « The next thing is: we can make IBM even better. We brought IBM back but we're gunning for leadership.» - Louis V. Gerstner, Jr.

#954 « I don't go by the rule book. I lead from the heart, not the head.» - Princess Diana

#955 « A leader leads by example not by Force.» - Sun Tzu

#956 « Leadership is particularly necessary to ensure ready acceptance of the unfamiliar and that which is contrary to tradition.» - Cyril Falls

#957 « France, after the month of May, will share trust with the current leadership of the United States which, on many subjects, has tended to take useful positions in our view.» - Francois Hollande

#958 « There is no force in the world that can block the powerful march of our army and people, who are holding high the banner of the suns of great Comrade Kim Il Sung and great Comrade Kim Jong Il and continuing to advance under the leadership of the party and with strong faith in sure victory.» - Kim Jong-un

#959 « The art of leadership... consists in consolidating the attention of the people against a single adversary and taking care that nothing will split up that attention.» - Adolf Hitler

#960 « Leadership should be born out of the understanding of the needs of those who would be affected by it.» - Marian Anderson

#961 « Leaders must encourage their organizations to dance to forms of music yet to be heard.» - Warren Bennis

#962 « Optimism is the ultimate definition of a leader. A leader has to look optimistically at what is ahead while not ignoring the challenges that must be overcome. Those challenges are in government, politics, world leadership, and even in community life.» - Linda McMahon

#963 « Great leaders do not desire to lead but to serve.» - Myles Munroe

#964 « I have always supported measures and principles and not men.» - Davy Crockett

#965 « Leadership is working with goals and vision; management is working with objectives.» - Russel Honore

#966 « Great leaders are not defined by the absence of weakness, but rather by the presence of clear strengths.» - John Zenger

#967 « Honor bespeaks worth. Confidence begets trust. Service brings satisfaction. Cooperation proves the quality of leadership.» - James Cash Penney

#968 « My focus as part of the leadership is to keep talking about the independent voters, independent voters - how do we get the independent voters back?» - Henry Cuellar

#969 « I think we so often equate leadership with being experts - the leader is supposed to come in and fix things. But in this interconnected world we live in now, it's almost impossible for just one person to do that.» - Jacqueline Novogratz

#970 « Leadership is a series of behaviors rather than a role for heroes.» - Margaret Wheatley

#971 « But the ability to articulate what you are doing, to be clear about it, and to stick to it is, I think, the essence of political leadership.» - Chris Patten

#972 « Our job... as we take forward this mantle of leadership as a new generation is to ensure that we not only bring our party back together, which has been bruised and battered this week, but that... we bring the parliament back together.» - Scott Morrison

#973 « The key to being a good manager is keeping the people who hate me away from those who are still undecided.» - Casey Stengel

#974 « There are two ways of spreading light: to be the candle or the mirror that reflects it.» - Edith Wharton

#975 « I am involved in a lot of nonprofits. And when I reached the ripe old age of 60, I wanted to provide leadership to some I had been involved in.» - David Rubenstein

#976 « Treat others the same way you want them to treat you.» - Luke 6:31

#977 « Seventy years after China emerged from the Second World War, the greatest threat facing the nation's leadership is not imperialism but skepticism.» - Evan Osnos

#978 « Not many of you should become teachers, my brothers, for you know that we who teach will be judged with greater strictness.» - James 3:1

#979 « A C.E.O.'s job is leadership, problem solving, and team building. I've done that my whole career.» - Bruce Rauner

#980 « Nothing so conclusively proves a man's ability to lead others as what he does from day to day to lead himself.» - Thomas J. Watson

#981 « Empowerment isn't a buzzword among leadership gurus. It's a proven technique where leaders give their teams the appropriate training, tools, resources, and guidance to succeed.» - John Rampton

#982 « Leadership in today's world requires far more than a large stock of gunboats and a hard fist at the conference table.» - Hubert H. Humphrey

#983 « Leaders don't force people to follow» - they invite them on a journey.

#984 « We all know business financial performance improves when more women are in senior levels of management and leadership.» - Beth Brooke

#985 « What's increasingly clear is that when you are open to a discussion of leadership, and you're relating it to your company, it is much easier to get people to become open.» - Kenneth Chenault

#986 « The very essence of leadership is that you have to have vision. You can't blow an uncertain trumpet.» - Theodore Hesburg

#987 « Leadership is about making the right decision and the best decision before, sometimes, it becomes entirely popular.» - Martin O'Malley

#988 « One of the surest signs of the estimated changes in the consciousness of the American proletariat is to be found in the character of the demands now being put forward by the leadership.» - C. L. R. James

#989 « You have no power at all if you do not exercise constant power.» - Major Owens

#990 « I think it is important for people who are given leadership roles to assume that role immediately.» - Bob Iger

#991 « Since joining the U.S. House of Representatives in November of 2006, I have strongly supported Speaker Nancy Pelosi. I have the utmost respect for her, and I believe the Democrats were able to accomplish a great deal under her leadership.» - Albio Sires

#992 « President Bush has shown great leadership. He has said that the 21st century will not be ruled or dictated by terrorists, dictators, and murderers. He is absolutely right. God bless him for his resolve.» - Lindsey Graham

#993 « To lead people, walk behind them.» - Lao Tzu

#994 « The union is much more than me, and when you think the union is you and it's not about who you represent, I think you've sort of lost your morals and focus and the purpose of your leadership.» - Andy Stern

#995 « There's a very big gulf between the black civil rights leadership in America and the black middle class in America. The black middle class are conservative. Many of those minorities can be persuaded to be members of the Republican Party.» - Pete du Pont

#996 « Before you are a leader, success is all about growing yourself. When you become a leader, success is all about growing others.» - Jack Welch

#997 « Management's job is to convey leadership's message in a compelling and inspiring way. Not just in meetings, but also by example.» - Jeffrey Gitomer

#998 « 'Start by doing what's necessary; then do what's possible; and suddenly you are doing the impossible.'» - Francis of Assisi

#999 « Taking on a leadership role doesn't mean that you only have to be personally ambitious.» - Jacinda Ardern

#1000 « If you judge people, you have no time to love them.» - Mother Teresa

#1001 « Sitting at a candidate rally is similar to sitting in a ballyard. Both give you the opportunity to assess the technical metrics and reflect on the intangibles - what baseball calls 'make up' and politics calls 'character' - the leadership, talent and maturity to add value to a venture.» - Christine Pelosi

#1002 « Earn your leadership every day.» - Michael Jordan

#1003 « Well football teams are perhaps easier to control than political parties, I'm sure the Prime Minister would agree with me, but yeah I think every team needs discipline and a sense of self-belief and that's important, that's what leadership's all about.» - Iain Duncan Smith

#1004 « Success is no longer about changing strategies more often, but having the agility to execute multiple strategies concurrently. And success requires CEOs to develop the right leadership capabilities, workforce skills, and corporate cultures to support digital transformation.» - Pierre Nanterme

#1005 « With gridlock the norm, Congress's approval rating is below 10 percent and the public has lost faith in its national leadership.» - Ron Fournier

#1006 « The more consistent a father can be or a mentor can be in the person's life and teach them principles of real solid manhood, character, integrity and leadership, the more consistent you can be in the person's life and teach them those things at a younger age, and then the better off they'll be.» - Allan Houston

#1007 « I think goals should never be easy, they should force you to work, even if they are uncomfortable at the time.» - Michael Phelps

#1008 « Leaders are visionaries with a poorly developed sense of fear and no concept of the odds against them.» - Robert Jarvik

#1009 « Since taking office, President Obama has worked to restore a positive vision of American leadership in the world - leadership defined, not by the threats and dangers that we will oppose, but by the security, opportunity and dignity that America advances in partnership with people around the world.» - John O. Brennan

#1010 « American presidential leadership never goes out of style.» - Monica Crowley

#1011 « You have to lead people gently toward what they already know is right.» - Phil Crosby

#1012 « People ask the difference between a leader and a boss. The leader leads, and the boss drives.» - Theodore Roosevelt

#1013 « The exercise of power is determined by thousands of interactions between the world of the powerful and that of the powerless, all the more so because these worlds are never divided by a sharp line: everyone has a small part of himself in both.» - Vaclav Havel

#1014 « When you can't make them see the light, make them feel the heat.» - Ronald Reagan

#1015 « Most businesses think that product is the most important thing, but without great leadership, mission and a team that deliver results at a high level, even the best product won't make a company successful.» - Robert Kiyosaki

#1016 « This week you will nominate the most experienced executive to seek the presidency in 60 years in Mitt Romney. He has no illusions about what makes America great, and he doesn't confuse the presidency with celebrity, or loftiness with leadership.» - Artur Davis

#1017 « Good leadership is to know when to go, and you only succeed as a good leader if you've transported someone else in and the company gets stronger. Then you've succeeded as leader.» - Tony Fernandes

#1018 « Whether it was his ability to turn around the Massachusetts economy or turn around businesses in the private sector, Mitt Romney has demonstrated the leadership that we need in the White House to get the country on the right track.» - Lisa Murkowski

#1019 « One of the joys of working with boys is that you get your pay as you go along. You can observe the results of your leadership daily... Such satisfaction cannot be purchased at any price; it must be earned.» - Ezra Taft Benson

#1020 « You take people as far as they will go, not as far as you would like them to go.» - Jeanette Rankin

#1021 « The first man gets the oyster, the second man gets the shell.» - Andrew Carnegie

#1022 « At a time when we are facing threats from nations such as North Korea and Iran, and attempting to convince others such as India and Pakistan to become responsible nuclear powers, it is vital that America reclaims the leadership we once had on arms control.» - Ellen Tauscher

#1023 « Hamas, also elected to governmental leadership in Palestine, includes the jihadists, people who have declared war on the United States of America and its ally, Israel.» - Zach Wamp

#1024 « An appreciative listener is always stimulating.» - Agatha Christie

#1025 « Integrity is a very important and an almost indispensable virtue that all leaders must possess. This is especially true in the Philippine context because we Filipinos really respond to leadership by example.» - Grace Poe

#1026 « Leadership is an action, not a position.» - Donald McGannon

#1027 « Be diligent to know the state of your flocks, And attend to your herds;» - Proverbs 27:23

#1028 « We have outstanding schools, world-class teaching and inspirational leadership across the country.» - Nicky Morgan

#1029 « You should set goals beyond your reach so you always have something to live for.» - Ted Turner

#1030 « Shouldn't Democrats insist that Sen. Durbin step down as their whip, the number two man in their leadership?» - Bill Kristol

#1031 « Leadership means not shying away from issues like safe abortion when the evidence shows us these services will save women's lives.» - Penny Mordaunt

#1032 « Arthur Scargill's leadership of the miners' strike has been a disgrace. The price to be paid for his folly will be immense. He will have destroyed the N.U.M. as an effective fighting force within British trade unionism for the next 20 years. If kamikaze pilots were to form their own union, Arthur would be an ideal choice for leader.» - Jimmy Reid

#1033 « What happened with Hurricane Katrina was the American electorate was forced to look at what lay behind the veneer of chest-beating. We all saw the consequences of having terrible government leadership.» - Susan Faludi

#1034 « Nobody rises to low expectations.» - Calvin Lloyd

#1035 « While President Obama assumes that at their core the Republican leadership team is just trying to do what's best for America, Mitch McConnell and John Boehner assume that the president is cynically trying to secure his own reelection, power, and legacy.» - Krystal Ball

#1036 « But I do not believe that the world would be entirely different if there were more women leaders. Maybe if everybody in leadership was a woman, you might not get into the conflicts in the first place. But if you watch the women who have made it to the top, they haven't exactly been non-aggressive - including me.» - Madeleine Albright

#1037 « This is one of the major problems we have. By the way, it was endorsed by leadership on both sides of the aisle and both ends of the Capitol, by the NRA and also by the gun control groups.» - John Dingell

#1038 « Ever since Israel has been a nation the United States has provided the leadership. Every president down to the ages has done this in a fairly balanced way, including George Bush senior, Gerald Ford, and others including myself and Bill Clinton.» - Jimmy Carter

#1039 « As long as the opposition believes the world will stand with Ukraine's democrat reformers, they will have the leverage and the courage to establish a legitimate republic under the leadership of Viktor Yushchenko.» - Bob Schaffer

#1040 « Leadership is inspiring extraordinary people to step up and serve their country.» - Justin Trudeau

#1041 « Often, sustainability is discussed only in the context of energy. Energy sustainability is essential - but the word has a much broader meaning. It means long-term thinking about how we manage our businesses, invest in social spending, and plan for the future. This requires vision and leadership, and it requires citizen engagement.» - Joe Kaeser

#1042 « The real leader has no need to lead - he is content to point the way.» - Henry Miller

#1043 « A winner is just a loser who tried one more time.» - George M. Moore Jr.

#1044 « Lincoln's leadership is based on a number of precepts, but my favorite one is that he acted in the name, and for the good, of the people.» - Steven Spielberg

#1045 « The employer generally gets the employees he deserves.» - J. Paul Getty

#1046 « Public office is supposed to be a public trust. This is a clear sign of the rampant corruption at the highest levels of the Republican leadership.» - Bob Etheridge

#1047 « A throne is only a bench covered with velvet.» - Napoleon Bonaparte

#1048 « Aren't we at the point where the closer we get to chaos, the more concern that there should be about coming to the table and compromising with Democrats? This is not leadership. This is almost like dictatorship.» - Debbie Wasserman Schultz

#1049 « All Americans and freedom-loving people around the world owe President Reagan our deepest gratitude for his strong, principled leadership that ended the Cold War and brought freedom to millions of people.» - Jim Ramstad

#1050 « You won't hear the leadership in the Republican Party admit it, but there are many in the House and Senate who know that illegal immigration has to be stopped and legal immigration has to be reduced. We are giving away the country so a few very rich people can get richer.» - Virgil Goode

#1051 « The key to successful leadership today is influence, not authority.» - Kenneth Blanchard

#1052 « The only thing that's keeping you from getting what you want is the story you keep telling yourself.» - Tony Robbins

#1053 « Ninety percent of leadership is the ability to communicate something people want.» - Dianne Feinstein

#1054 « I don't want to over generalize, but I believe that women are typically drawn to leadership styles that focus on consensus building, effective listening and working in teams. That's certainly been my leadership style, and I think it's been very successful.» - Margaret Hamburg

#1055 « To meet the expectations of the majority of our people, and to open up new vistas of economic opportunity so that the aspirations of Nigerians can stand a fair chance of being fulfilled in a lifetime, there must be a truly committed leadership in a democratic Nigeria.» - Ibrahim Babangida

#1056 « The person who says it cannot be done should not interrupt the person who is doing it.» - Chinese Proverb

#1057 « And I'd say one of the great lessons I've learned over the past couple of decades, from a management perspective, is that really when you come down to it, it really is all about people and all about leadership.» - Steve Case

#1058 « I think America has more than enough maturity and intelligence to start exercising its world leadership responsibly.» - Cristina Kirchner

#1059 « Leaders must be close enough to relate to others, but far enough ahead to motivate them.» - John C. Maxwell

#1060 « Denmark needs change, Denmark needs to move on and Denmark needs my leadership.» - Helle Thorning-Schmidt

#1061 « Time is neutral and does not change things. With courage and initiative, leaders change things.» - Jesse Jackson

#1062 « Leadership consists not in degrees of technique but in traits of character; it requires moral rather than athletic or intellectual effort, and it imposes on both leader and follower alike the burdens of self-restraint.» - Lewis H. Lapham

#1063 « You have to have your heart in the business and the business in your heart.» - An Wang

#1064 « Pay attention to those employees who respectfully ask why. They are demonstrating an interest in their jobs and exhibiting a curiosity that could eventually translate into leadership ability.» - Harvey Mackay

#1065 « Leaders have to act more quickly today. The pressure comes much faster.» - Andy Grove

#1066 « He who is slow to anger is better than the mighty, And he who rules his spirit than he who takes a city.» - Proverbs 16:32

#1067 « We were hoping Obama would reclaim moral leadership for America. That failed.» - Lech Walesa

#1068 « There are very good people in the Labour Party who I would like to see in leadership.» - Betty Boothroyd

#1069 « Party domination and State leadership are concepts incompatible with one another.» - Franz von Papen

#1070 « Our doubts are traitors, and make us lose the good we oft might win, by fearing to attempt.» - William Shakespeare

#1071 « Most leadership strategies are doomed to failure from the outset. As people have been noting for years, the majority of strategic initiatives that are driven from the top are marginally effective - at best.» - Peter Senge

#1072 « I believe that the will of the people is resolved by a strong leadership. Even in a democratic society, events depend on a strong leadership with a strong power of persuasion, and not on the opinion of the masses.» - Yitzhak Shamir

#1073 « I have always supported measures and principles and not men.» - Davy Crockett

#1074 « It's very important in a leadership role not to place your ego at the foreground and not to judge everything in relationship to how your ego is fed.» - Ruth J. Simmons

#1075 « If I were not African, I wonder whether it would be clear to me that Africa is a place where the people do not need limp gifts of fish but sturdy fishing rods and fair access to the pond. I wonder whether I would realize that while African nations have a failure of leadership, they also have dynamic people with agency and voices.» - Chimamanda Ngozi Adichie

#1076 « The world is yearning for strong leadership and moral clarity; someone who knows the difference between good and bad.» - Isaac Herzog

#1077 « My observation is that women are merely waiting for their husbands to assume leadership.» - James Dobson

#1078 « Look over your shoulder now and then to be sure someone's following you.» - Henry Gilmer

#1079 « I want to use my position of leadership to help move along at a faster pace what I believe and know the Obama administration wants to do around the urgency of climate change.» - Kamala Harris

#1080 « I think people are worried about leadership and me being a pretty quiet guy. But I would say I'm not too quiet. I'll talk your ear off.» - Justin Herbert

#1081 « My leadership will end the Obama era and begin a new era of American prosperity.» - Mitt Romney

#1082 « Leadership is an individual sport, one that has to be fine-tuned to each of the people that reports to you. Leaders also need to provide the direction, energy, encouragement and inspiration for each person who reports directly to the leader as well as for the overall organization.» - David Petraeus

#1083 « I don't know any other way to lead but by example.» - Don Shula

#1084 « Globalisation means many other countries are asserting themselves and trying to take over leadership. Please don't ask Americans to let others assume the leadership of human exploration. We can do wonderful science on the Moon, and wonderful commercial things. Then we can pack up and move on to Mars.» - Buzz Aldrin

#1085 « In the past, the U.S. has shown its capacity to reinvent its gifts for leadership. During the 1970s, in the aftermath of the Nixon abdication and the Ford and Carter presidencies, the whole nation peered into the abyss, was horrified by what it saw and elected Ronald Reagan as president, which began a national resurgence.» - Paul Johnson

#1086 « President Clinton not only benefits by gay and lesbian votes, but he benefits by showing the nation that he is a strong leader who implements his beliefs, who stands firm by those who he believes are being treated unfairly, and I think people respect that kind of leadership in the country.» - David Mixner

#1087 « Get the best people and train them well.» - Scott McNealy

#1088 « Do or do not. There is no try.» - Yoda

#1089 « To lead the people, walk behind them.» - Lao

#1090 « And this administration and this House leadership have said, quote-unquote, they will stop at nothing to pass this health care bill. And now they've gotten rid of me and it will pass. You connect the dots.» - Eric Massa

#1091 « The nicest thing about standards is that there are so many of them to choose from.» - Ken Olsen

#1092 « Keep your fears to yourself, but share your courage with others.» - Robert L. Stevenson

#1093 « I think for me, or for anyone who plays the quarterback position, it's almost an unspoken word when you think about leadership. Some guys can be a leader and be a running back or a lineman, or wide receiver, strong safety, or linebacker. But when you speak of quarterbacks, it's automatically a default that you're supposed to be a leader.» - Cam Newton

#1094 « For women to achieve equal representation in leadership roles, it's important that they have the backing of men as well as women.» - Adam Grant

#1095 « There is a great man who makes every man feel small. But the real great man is the man who makes every man feel great.» - G.K. Chesterton

#1096 « Within the narrow confines of Permanent Washington - the journalists, lobbyists, and congressional lifers who are the city's avatars of centrism and continuity - Ford is considered the beau ideal of American leadership.» - Timothy Noah

#1097 « You don't lead by hitting people over the head» - that's assault, not leadership. - Dwight D. Eisenhower

#1098 « Character matters; leadership descends from character.» - Rush Limbaugh

#1099 « How the hell can I ask people who work for me to travel cheaply if I travel in luxury? It's a question of good leadership.» - Ingvar Kamprad

#1100 « In the '90s, there was scant presidential leadership and insufficient domestic political mobilization for foreign policy grounded in human rights.» - Samantha Power

#1101 « To command is to serve, nothing more and nothing less.» - Andre Malraux

#1102 « Lead from the back» - and let others believe they are in front.

#1103 « I work closely with Hispanic leadership.» - Gene Green

#1104 « Instead of starting a new nuclear arms race, now is the time to reclaim our Nation's position of leadership on nuclear nonproliferation efforts.» - Dianne Feinstein

#1105 « I think the most important leadership lessons I've learned have to do with understanding the context in which you are leading. Universities are places with enormously distributed authority and many different sorts of constituencies, all of whom have a stake in that institution.» - Drew Gilpin Faust

#1106 « Charlatanism of some degree is indispensable to effective leadership.» - Eric Hoffer

#1107 « Everything you've ever wanted is on the other side of fear.» - George Addair

#1108 « I had a sense of what leadership meant and what it could do for you. So am I surprised that I am sitting up here on the 62nd floor of Rockefeller Plaza? No.» - Vernon Jordan

#1109 « But the fact is that the vast majority of Republicans support the Sinn Fein leadership.» - Martin McGuinness

#1110 « Bad leadership during the past years has cast on our Party the shadow of great and grave burdens.» - Janos Kadar

#1111 « Optimism is the faith that leads to achievement. Nothing can be done without hope and confidence.» - Helen Keller

#1112 « Absolute identity with one's cause is the first and great condition of successful leadership.» - Woodrow Wilson

#1113 « Believe you can and you're halfway there.» - Theodore Roosevelt

#1114 « A good leader leads the people from above them. A great leader leads the people from within them.» - M.D. Arnold

#1115 « It is better to have a lion at the head of an army of sheep, than a sheep at the head of an army of lions.» - Daniel Defoe

#1116 « Anyone can hold the helm when the sea is calm.» - Publilius Syrus

#1117 « Projecting weakness will not make us safer or discourage attacks against us. We need to show leadership and strength by demonstrating that we will not tolerate violent acts against our people, and we will not leave our citizens or our interests vulnerable to an attack.» - Tom Rooney

#1118 « Very often, we think of leadership being at the very top of an organisation. I think what's unique about ABG is that we have a very strong cadre of leaders across the organisation who are highly empowered and therefore play a very major role in the growth and evolution of the organization.» - Kumar Mangalam Birla

#1119 « I fully support U.N. Secretary General Ban Ki-moon in his Global Education First Initiative and the work of U.N. Special Envoy for Global Education Gordon Brown and the respectful president of the U.N. General Assembly Vuk Jeremic. I thank them for the leadership they continue to give.» - Malala Yousafzai

#1120 « Leadership does not depend on being right.» - Ivan Illich

#1121 « When we can export American energy to markets around the world, the president will also be able to use it as an important tool to increase our global leadership and influence, advancing our global agenda and helping to keep our citizens safe.» - Sarah Huckabee Sanders

#1122 « I suppose leadership at one time meant muscles; but today it means getting along with people.» - Mahatma Gandhi

The Importance of Inspirational Leadership in Fostering Growth and Success

Leadership is a dynamic and ever-evolving process that requires constant learning, adaptation, and improvement. To become an effective leader, one must cultivate a deep sense of empathy, resilience, and vision. The collection of 1122 quotes in this book offers valuable insights, practical advice, and timeless wisdom from some of the greatest leaders in history.

Through the power of language, these quotes can inspire and empower individuals to become better leaders, build stronger teams, and achieve greater success. Whether you are a seasoned executive, a middle manager, or a new supervisor, the wisdom in this book can help you navigate the challenges of leadership with grace and confidence.

One of the key themes that emerges from the quotes in this book is the importance of self-awareness and emotional intelligence. Effective leaders are those who are able to connect with others on a deeper level, understand their own strengths and weaknesses, and cultivate a sense of purpose that inspires and motivates their teams. By developing these qualities, leaders can create a culture of trust, respect, and collaboration that drives organizational success.

Ultimately, the journey of leadership is a lifelong one that requires ongoing commitment, dedication, and humility. As the quotes in this book remind us, there is no one-size-fits-all approach to leadership, and no leader is perfect. However, by embracing the lessons and insights offered in this book, you can become a more effective, inspiring, and compassionate leader who makes a positive impact on your team and your organization.

Printed in Great Britain
by Amazon